T0329631

The Making of a Market

JULIETTE LEVY

The Making of a Market

Credit, Henequen, and Notaries
in Yucatán, 1850–1900

THE PENNSYLVANIA STATE UNIVERSITY PRESS
UNIVERSITY PARK, PENNSYLVANIA

Library of Congress Cataloging-in-Publication Data

Levy, Juliette, 1968–
The making of a market : credit, henequen, and notaries
in Yucatán, 1850–1900 / Juliette Levy.
p. cm.
Includes bibliographical references and index.
Summary: "Examines the functioning of credit markets
in Mexico, through the agency of notaries, during the
Yucatán region's nineteenth-century henequen export
boom. Explores the mobilization of capital and the
creation of credit markets before banks existed"—
Provided by publisher.
ISBN 978-0-271-05213-7 (cloth : alk. paper)
1. Credit—Mexico—Yucatán (State).
2. Notaries—Mexico—Yucatán (State)—History—
19th century.
3. Yucatán (Mexico : State)—Economic conditions—
19th century.
4. Henequen (Plant)—Mexico—Yucatán (State).
I. Title.

HG3701.L48 2012
332.70972'6509034—dc23
2011031594

The Pennsylvania State University Press is a member of the
Association of American University Presses.

It is the policy of The Pennsylvania State University Press
to use acid-free paper. Publications on uncoated stock
satisfy the minimum requirements of American National
Standard for Information Sciences—Permanence of Paper
for Printed Library Material, ANSI Z39.48–1992.

This book is printed on Natures Natural,
which contains 50% post-consumer waste.

Contents

Figures and Tables

Figures

Tables

Acknowledgments

No matter what you say, there's some debts you never pay.
—Arcade Fire, "Intervention"

Writing this book was both an exploration of its subject and a personal reminder of the many people, institutions, and networks that support and encourage productivity. It really does take a village of advisors, archivists, librarians, colleagues, friends, family, and a dog or two to write a book.

The book, its revisions, and its final form would have been impossible without the help, comments, close readings, and questions of Naomi Lamoreaux and Jean-Laurent Rosenthal. I also owe more than I will ever be able to repay to Catherine Allgor, Gustavo del Ángel-Mobarak, Alessandro Fornazzari, Adrián García-Mosqueira, Ann Goldberg, Aurora Gómez-Galvarriato, Anne Hanley, Randolph C. Head, Laura Lewis, Ghislaine Lydon, Aldo Musacchio, Freya Schiwy, Susan Silver, Stephanie Smith, Gail Triner, Mary Yeager, and Fariba Zarinebaf. They, together with my colleagues and the staff of the History Department at the University of California, Riverside, all provided intellectual and emotional support at crucial intersections. Similar thanks go out to Sandy Thatcher and the editorial and publishing staff of Penn State University Press.

One person to whom I owe more than just thanks is no longer with us to read this acknowledgment. I will always be grateful to, and miss, Ken Sokoloff.

My experience in the Yucatán archives would have been decidedly more difficult were it not for Susi Peniche and the staff of the Archivo Notarial del Estado de Yucatán and the Archivo General del Estado de Yucatán. At the Biblioteca Menéndez and the Asociación Genealógica de Yucatán, I owe special thanks to the director of the collection, Licenciado Peón Ancona, who aided in accessing the parish records of the archdiocese of Yucatán. Doña Beatriz Heredia de Pau and Faulo Sánchez Novelo at the Centro de Apoyo a la Investigación Histórica de Yucatán were both helpful guides and very kind hosts.

In Mexico City, I am grateful to Veronica Aguilar at the Biblioteca de la Escuela de Notarios and to the reference desk staff at the Archivo General de la Nación.

Institutional support is equally important, if not crucial, and I cannot imagine writing a book without the support of the excellent staff of librarians I have met. The UCLA Young Research Library in Los Angeles was home for many a weekend, as was the Linfield College Library in McMinnville, Oregon, where Susan Barnes Whyte and her staff provided access to reference literature and a quiet respite. I was a fellow at the Kellogg Institute for International Studies at the University of Notre Dame, where I started the work of transforming a dissertation into a book. The University of California, Riverside, has been very generous, and a stint at its Riverside Center for Ideas and Society helped me further. The UC-Presidential Fellowship in the Humanities gave me time and resources to finish revising the manuscript. I am also grateful to the *Hispanic American Historical Review* and the *Business History Review* for letting me use previously published material. Material from chapter 5 appears here by permission of the *Hispanic American Historical Review* and Duke University Press, and material from chapter 6 is used by permission of the *Business History Review* and Harvard University Press.

Ultimately, the relationships outside of the academic cordon sustained me most and rewarded me amply—my friends and family in Brussels, Mexico City, New York, Berkeley, Los Angeles, and Oregon—you all know who you are, and you know I couldn't have done it without you.

Last and absolutely not least, I owe so much to David Millman—husband, friend, partner, and never-ending font of encouragement, insight, wit, and love. This one is for you.

Chapter One

Introduction

In developed capital markets, financial intermediaries and banks have almost become synonymous. Today, people deposit their savings with banks, make use of their payment facilities, invest through their brokerage offices, get cash at electronic tellers, and apply for mortgages by filling out standardized forms. Banks are ubiquitous financial institutions today, but they are a relatively recent phenomenon.[1] In Mexico, before the existence of banks in the late nineteenth century, nonbank financial intermediaries handled most of the financial tasks we associate with banks. For all we know about banks, we still know very little about how the intermediaries that predate them functioned and who precisely they were. For example, absent specific formation charters, how did they become intermediaries in the first place, and what circumstances—be they legal, political, economic, or simply accidental—put them in a position to provide financial intermediation and to do so in such a way as to influence and create markets?

These questions are all the more relevant in markets where economic growth happened without banks—which is Yucatán's story and the topic of this book. Yucatán, like many regions in Latin America, experienced a protracted economic boom during the nineteenth century. Foreign demand for henequen, a local cordage fiber, stimulated the economy out of its postcolonial slump. Henequen had been used as naval cordage in the early nineteenth century and became the preferred binding twine in mechanical wheat binders in the United States and Canada in the late nineteenth century. Fueled by this demand for a primary good that was almost exclusive to the region, modern Yucatán transformed from a cattle-ranching and subsistence-farming society into a booming export-oriented agricultural economy.

In the context of Yucatán's nineteenth-century agricultural boom, this book studies how credit markets worked before the emergence of modern banks. The boom occurred without the assistance of modern financial institutions; instead, mortgage loans arranged through local notaries raised the capital that land owners and merchants invested in crops and infrastructure. The importance of these informal or personal credit markets in supporting productive activities that generated growth and development is not surprising for early modern societies in which tradespeople, individuals, and religious institutions advanced loans.[2] The novelty of the Yucatán case is that personal credit networks continued to be important in the nineteenth century and were very quickly mobilized through the person of the notary to finance one of the major commodity booms in Latin American history.

This finding challenges the notion that large-scale investment capital could be mobilized only through formal financial institutions or through specialized enterprises directly engaged in the henequen trade. Yucatán changed from a regional backwater into a participant in the global cordage market, and it did so without any local banks. While foreign brokers extended trade loans to the most important producers and traders of henequen, all other participants in the local economy carried Yucatán from its colonial past into modernity by relying on traditional forms of personal finance.

Even though personal credit was probably the major source of credit in most countries before the twentieth century, we know little about how these personal mortgage markets worked in Latin America. Historical research on credit markets has focused on banks, and economic historians have privileged these institutional histories and assumed that informal markets did not support a large enough part of the market. The case of Yucatán analyzed here overturns this assumption.

This book provides an analysis of how intermediaries mobilized personal credit markets through the office of notaries, many of which became unwitting catalysts of Yucatán's capitalist transformation. It provides a crucial addition to the historiography of formal institutional finance, showing that interpersonal credit markets operated before the creation of banks and that notaries were crucial financial intermediaries. In Yucatán's personal, local, and small credit market, notaries embodied trust, monitored reputations, managed networks, and provided social enforcement to support the flow of credit. This example of economic growth supported by financial intermediaries demonstrates that additional and important sources of credit can exist before and, perhaps most importantly, without banks.

Economic Growth

Latin America's development lag compared to the United States or Europe has occupied historians for quite some time, and the explanations draw a picture of a development process marred by the colonial experience.[3] Historians and economists have traced economic, ethnic, and political inequality back to patterns established and reinforced by the colonial system. However, it is difficult to connect modern transformations, or the lack thereof, to the colonial period alone, and the colonial legacy certainly cannot explain the different patterns of financial development among Latin American countries after independence from Spain and Portugal.

Independence did unshackle Mexico from the straitjacket of colonial commercial restraints. The progressive purpose of many of its postindependence presidents was to catch up with Europe and leave the colonial legacy behind. Both conservatives and liberals were dedicated to reinvigorating Mexico's economic position and reclaiming a place in the global trade network, which Mexico had lost when it separated from Spain. The political instability and conflict between political factions probably delayed this economic revival in the nineteenth century, but Mexico, like many other Latin American countries, benefited from a primary goods export boom fueled by the industrialization of the other parts of the world. In this context of national rebuilding and economic revival, the development of financial markets and institutions would become critical.

Financial development and economic growth are irrevocably connected (financial innovation and economic innovation both contribute to growth), and this suggests that the growth booms in Latin America should have given birth to a series of financial institutions geared toward supporting the allocation of savings and investments that traditionally fund credit. This did in fact happen, as state-chartered banks opened throughout the Americas in the nineteenth century, starting with the Banco Comercial de Río de Janeiro and the Banco do Brasil in 1851.[4] The two merged in 1853 to form the first and largest institution of commercial credit in Latin America. Also in this period the Argentinian government established the charter of operations for its Banco de la Provincia de Buenos Aires, the first locally funded and managed bank in Argentina, which became the first bank to issue long-term residential loans in 1856.

In Mexico the first Mexican private banks were formed even later, during Emperor Maximilian's reign (1864–67), but these banks functioned more as royal treasuries than as modern banks. Prior to these, the Banco de Avío was created by the government in 1830 to support infant industry, but it closed some fifteen years later. Other preexisting banks were foreign owned and operated and functioned as investment banks or trade credit providers (as was the case of the English Banco de Londres, México, y Sudamérica). It was not until President Porfirio Díaz's long term in office that private banks became an important part of the Mexican financial system. The Banco de Santa Eulalia, chartered in 1875, was the first; the Banco Nacional de México, chartered in 1882, was the most important. In late nineteenth-century Mexico, the Banco de México had almost exclusive note-issuance privileges, managed the government's budget, and was in charge of servicing the government's domestic and foreign debt; it has been argued that it acted like Mexico's de facto banker of last resort.[5] Regional banks also expanded during this period, and Yucatán's henequen traders followed suit and opened two banks in 1889.

Yucatán's growth predates the birth of local banks in 1889, and henequen had been harvested and processed on local plantations in increasing amounts since the middle of the century. Given that banks did not finance that expansion, that foreign brokers mostly financed trade, and that henequen plants had a seven-year seed-to-plant maturation time, how did the Yucatecan economy finance its long-term investments?

To answer this question we need to think of the financial role of institutions and actors that are not banks. Banks are only the most recent embodiment of financial institutions, and the focus on banks as vehicles of economic growth obscures the fact that debt was ubiquitous well before the creation of banks. From the commitment letters of eleventh-century Maghribi traders to trading debts of Spanish merchants in New Spain and the mundane debts of eighteenth- and nineteenth-century English parishioners, there is reliable and plentiful evidence of active credit markets throughout the world that existed without banks.[6] This was doubly true in nineteenth-century Yucatán, where the demand for henequen and the lack of banks promoted the growth of a market for personal loans. The notarial ledgers maintained in the Yucatán archives confirm that credit markets do not require banks to exist. They also reveal that notaries, not banks, were the financial intermediaries that responded to the demands of local economic growth. What the market needed wasn't necessarily banks, but the existence of financial intermediaries that could perform the functions that banks eventually internalized.

The literature on Yucatán has focused justifiably on the role of trading houses and import-export houses such as Escalante y Compañía and Molina y Compañía. These institutions preceded banks and were created to support those involved in the henequen trade, to whom they advanced large sums of capital each planting season and on behalf of whom they negotiated with foreign purchasers over the price of henequen in return for product.[7] The trading houses were crucial in the global reach of henequen, and they structured the market in ways very advantageous to them—thereby guaranteeing a majority share in both the business sphere and the politics of Yucatán. As financial intermediaries, however, the trading houses were relative latecomers and imperfect coordinators. Trading houses lent exclusively to planters that could repay them in fiber, which excluded smaller planters and anyone not borrowing for a henequen plantation.

The financial intermediaries that supported the early growth of the henequen boom as well as the expansion of the credit market beyond the strict limits of the henequen producers were the notaries, who sit at the heart of this book and at the intersection of market norms and social norms.[8] They facilitated contact between borrowers and lenders without doing any lending themselves, and in doing so, their intermediary role was closely tied to their social role. The role of notaries is often overlooked in this context, and they deserve to be analyzed in depth to reinterpret and recast their place in society and history as well as in the functioning of an economy.

This book steps away from the traditional emphasis on banks in financial studies and reconceptualizes the financial market through the role of intermediaries. In shifting the perspective from formal financial institutions to notaries, the book joins a body of research on informal relations in markets—part of a growing scholarship that studies informal mechanisms of credit distribution and demonstrates the importance of such mechanisms in developing economies.[9]

Financial Intermediation

The roles performed by notaries in financial markets position the notaries firmly as a link between the economy inherited from the Spaniards and

Mexico's modern financial system. As embodiments of the civic trust, notaries recorded the transactions that trace Mexico's capitalist transformation from Spanish colony to independent republic. The trust embodied in the notarial institution and the informal nature of the networks in which notaries worked underscores the importance of informal institutions and traditional mechanisms of trust in the transition to modernity.

Time-honored figures in the Spanish and French legal tradition of recording civil transactions, notaries were the main contact between civil society and the body of laws imposed by successive governments in colonial and independent Mexico.[10] Notaries were a source of stability throughout the changes in governance and laws. They continued their record-keeping tasks no matter what the political, economic, or diplomatic circumstance, as their core activities were relatively impervious to wars and revolutions. As a historical documentary source, notaries provide a privileged perspective into the reverberations of social, political, and economic upheavals.

The constancy of notarial activity is particularly useful when studying economic markets during the tumultuous nineteenth century. Mexico was wracked with political infighting, as the conflict between the centralist liberals and the federalist conservatives erupted in civil wars. The first half of the century was a period during which Mexico faced secession both in the north and in the south. Texas seceded successfully in 1836 and Yucatán tried but failed in 1844. Invasions, both by the United States as well as European powers, followed.

It was a period of economic distress (especially in the immediate aftermath of independence) and economic rebound. It was also a period of legal reform and political exploration. Mexico started the nineteenth century as a colony, was twice an empire and, depending on how they are counted, supported about seventy-five separate presidencies.[11] In the midst of this chaos, notaries recorded contracts and continued to perform their civic duties, continued to be not just the pillar of civil contracting but a bulwark against the changing political and economic landscape.

The Mexican independence wars were a significant shock to the Mexican economy, most obviously on the rates of economic growth and the level of exports and trade with Mexico's traditional European trade partners. The recovery from these losses and the imposition of calm under Porfirio Díaz are part of the great successes and contradictions of this period in Mexico's history. And below the surface of the political conflicts and rearrangements, informal institutions and intermediaries weathered the shocks and continued operating. In Mexico City, for example, pawnshops, one of the oldest operating short-term credit providers, did not stop during the independence wars or the revolution in the early twentieth century.[12] This was also the case for the mortgage market in Yucatán during the period covered in this book. Notaries oversaw the private credit market and recorded private mortgages with interest rates that reflected changes in laws and perceived risks in the markets, operating for all intents and purposes like financial brokers. Mortgage banks, on the other hand, had to wait until the last decade of the nineteenth century to get a charter and begin operating in the Yucatán Peninsula.

Contrary to notaries, banks first started operating in Mérida, the capital of Yucatán, in the late nineteenth century, and for the better part of the henequen boom, credit was privately allocated through long-term collateralized credit in the form of mortgage loans. Save for foreign-trade credit (reserved for large traders during the boom) and pawnshop credit (in smaller amounts but among a larger proportion of the population), such loans could be legal and enforceable only if they were recorded in a notary's office and carried the notarial seal.[13] Even after banks opened in Yucatán, their lending terms were limited, and while foreign brokerage houses provided longer-term loans for henequen production and export, these loans were limited to all but the biggest producers. The last and often only option for secured credit during the nineteenth century was the mortgage loan or contract (I often refer to them as "mortgages" throughout the book).

In this setting where land was wealth and banks did not exist, mortgage credit became the single and most widely used mechanism to raise long-term debt. This does not discount the role of other credit sources, but it does emphasize the widespread use and deep reliance on long-term mortgage credit. In Yucatán, mortgages financed mostly agricultural ventures, and there is evidence that the use of mortgages to finance productive activity was not limited to Yucatán. The textile industry in the state of Veracruz also used mortgage credit to finance itself in the nineteenth century.[14] And beyond Mexico, mortgages also fueled the French financial and industrial markets in the eighteenth and nineteenth centuries.[15]

Nineteenth-Century Economic History

The importance of mortgages and nontraditional financial intermediaries has received relatively little attention because, traditionally, financial institutions and development in Latin America has been analyzed in comparison to the economic histories of Europe and the United States. Modern institutional deposit and investment banks are a feature of European and U.S. economic history, and the delay in development in other parts of the world has been analyzed through the prism of the standards that have come before them. This perspective has skewed our view of markets in the developing world, leading many to ask why banks in Mexico, Morocco, or Malaysia, for example, did not arise at the same time, play the same role, or provide the same impetus to growth as they did in Western Europe and the United States.

Today, many scholars of Latin American financial development are reversing this trend and studying local development without relying on these traditional comparisons. Gail Triner advances our understanding of banks and the intricacy of their corporate governance in Brazil, and Aldo Musacchio overturns many assumptions about the effect of the colonial legacy on Brazilian economic development, much as Leonor Ludlow, Carlos Marichal, Steve Haber, Gustavo del Ángel-Mobarak, and Noel Maurer have done for Mexico.[16] Steve Haber's more recent analysis of the commitments that tie governments to bank stakeholders and compel them to honor their mutual obligations complicates our understanding of the logic of Latin American financial markets.[17] These are all pioneering works, especially in their break with the theoretical and empirical legacy of the dependency school. Together, these recent studies chart a new course for Latin American economic history of credit, yet they still maintain a perspective that defines it as the history of banks and public finance.[18]

That said, the literature on banking and finance in Latin America also agrees that local and informal credit relations were necessary for the creation and development of a national banking network.[19] Anne Hanley has demonstrated that local networks were at the origin of the sophisticated financial institutions that marked Brazil's late nineteenth-century economy and that the demands of the coffee trade combined with the end of slavery were not alone in supporting the Brazilian financial markets; coffee traders (or coffee *factors*, as they are known) and local debt markets supported the existence of these markets before they became national, formal, and modern.[20]

Historians studying the colonial period focus, by default, on nonbank intermediaries. They study the importance of traders and the church in the development of colonial markets and provide insight into the functioning of premodern credit markets.[21] With his sweeping analysis of the Guadalajara region in the eighteenth century, Eric Van Young demonstrates that regional studies can have an explanatory impact for the rest of the area. His research determines that urban trade and agricultural production in the colonial period depended on each other not just for commodity production and sale but also for the longer-term financial needs of both. Van Young's and Linda Greenow's detailed studies of credit in colonial Mexico describe the overlap and dependence between producers, traders, and financers, and although neither articulates the role of intermediaries, they introduce a clear picture of socially embedded commercial interactions and a fledgling, if unidentified, role for informal intermediaries.[22]

Financial and economic studies of the immediate postindependence period are few, most likely because, except for Brazil, most Latin American economies were mostly in disarray. At the national level, Barbara Tenenbaum studies the pitiful state of public finance during the revolving governments of the early independent period and shows that chaos was the one constant in this period. Margaret Chowning's work on Michoacán demonstrates that not all regions in Mexico experienced the conflicts and resolutions that marked the national scene in the same way.[23] Independence freed Mexico from the weight of the colonial regime but did not replace it with anything firm or reliable.

The resulting power vacuum had two sets of consequences. First, Mexico's governments were led by a revolving door of presidents, dictators, and one foreign emperor, while the colonial structure was replaced with a semifunctional independent alternative. Second, in the absence of trustworthy public institutions, personal wealth and power became achievable and noticeable goals. The historical record of the nineteenth century is long on chaos and large family fortunes, and the survival of these regional family fortunes is a pillar of nineteenth-century studies. David Walker's and Alex Saragoza's studies of kinship and wealth in the nineteenth century hint at the role of informal relations in markets and argue in favor of the family and kinship networks as agents of these markets.[24]

Families and the reliance on kinship networks in Latin America have often been used to explain its economic development lag—especially in the case of Yucatán, where the mythical power of the "Casta Divina" overshadows many of the studies of the henequen boom. The Casta Divina is the term used to refer to a group of wealthy families who owned a significant share of the land and wielded considerable political power in nineteenth-century Yucatán. The Molina clan, the Peón family, the Cámaras, and the Escalantes dominated politics and trade, and their existence has served to reinforce the fact that in Yucatán, as in the rest of Mexico, family networks, interlocking business directorates, and other forms of insider lending were a response to a lack of trust in and the pervasive weakness of the legal and governmental institutions.[25] The argument that kinship networks and preexisting institutions were at the root of the inefficiencies in the economic system of Mexico has great explanatory thrust, but the existence of overlapping family connections in business cannot prove that it was the driving force. The evidence from the mortgage market in Yucatán suggests that kin was not necessarily king. This point has been made by economic sociologists who recognize and demonstrate that intangible elements such as trust can hold more value than any material or familial bond—and that the less obvious ties (the ones Mark Granovetter calls "weak") may be the ones holding the network together.[26]

Apart from kinship and delayed financial development, property rights also address the delay in the development of financial markets in Latin America, especially in the context of poverty and political instability. Douglass North best articulates the effect that legal constraints could have on economic activity in the United States and Europe, but no one has illustrated it more convincingly for Latin America than Hernando de Soto. De Soto recognizes the static property rights of land ownership in Peru as an obstacle to the development of credit markets and a cause of poverty in the countryside. In the Peruvian twentieth-century context, de Soto identifies this as a leading cause of terrorism and instability. Like de Soto, historians of the Mexican Revolution made the connection between the massive land privatizations of the nineteenth century and the revolution, but de Soto's work provides a theoretical and empirical context in which to conceptualize the problem.[27] The exclusion of different constituencies from credit markets, and markets in general, can benefit greatly from being understood as a consequence of property rights regimes. Bringing this back to Yucatán, the absence of ethnic Mayas from the mortgage market and the conditions under which women participated is best understood as a reflection of market responses to their truncated property rights, rather than as a response to ethnic bias or sexism.

Notarial Sources

Because of notaries' integral role in the judicial system (contrary to law-yers, who had no obligation to record their transactions), notaries recorded all civil agreements and contracts, as well as the detailed notes of those agreements between their clients. As a consequence, notarial records are a staple of historical research, and many historians have used the mundane details of personal life that notaries recorded.[28] The term "notary" in fact springs etymologically from this very act of "taking note," an act per-formed diligently throughout the ages. The tasks they performed per their mandated functions and the records that notaries left behind are the mate-rial with which one can thoroughly document the history of the mundane acts that constitute a society's interactions.

The collaborative work of Philip Hoffman, Gilles Postel-Vinay, and Jean-Laurent Rosenthal, as well as research by Julie Hardwick and Donna Merwick, all rely on notaries' copious notes to study their subjects and the world in which they operate.[29] These scholars have reclaimed the role of the notary by recasting him respectively as the servant of financial innova-tion, the embodiment of middling patriarchs, and one of the casualties of the British conquest of New York. Jointly, they rewrite history from the perspective of a humble civil servant. In the Netherlands, notaries are also the subject of renewed interest because the financial accounts they re-corded and managed are an important gateway to understanding the local effects of the economic growth in the Low Lands during the heyday of exploration and foreign trade (through the Dutch East India Company, for example). Among the Latin Americanists, Kathryn Burns, Catherine LeGrand, and Adriana Mercedes Corso have seen notaries as influential participants in the mundane worlds of colonial Peru and nineteenth-century Colombia.[30] In all their works, as well as in this book, notaries are not just the providers of documentary sources; they are the main subjects of research.

The records used here were collected in the State Archive of Yucatán (Archivo General del Estado de Yucatán; AGEY) and its Notarial Archive (Archivo Notarial del Estado de Yucatán; ANEY). The data set comprises all the mortgage contracts that were recorded in the surviving ledgers between 1850 and 1900. I use every mortgage that was recorded in the ledgers from 1850, 1860, 1870, 1875, 1880, 1885, 1890, and 1895. Because sampling throughout the years would have complicated the assessment of the secular growth of the mortgage market, every mortgage contract recorded in every surviving notarial ledger in the Notarial Archive and the State Archive of Yucatán in the eight benchmark years are part of the data set. The data consists of approximately 1,000 contracts and also includes a subset of mortgages that were recorded by one of Mérida's most important notaries, José Anacleto Patrón Zavalegui. His data set of 448 mortgages includes every mortgage contract he recorded between 1875 and 1899.

Another part of the data set consists of the debts that were recorded in more than 300 probate records. This part of the data set consists of 337 estate inventories from 1847 to 1901 and includes 128 probates from Maya decedents. These postmortem accounts are reliable documents for wealth estimates, as long as one acknowledges the inherent bias in probates, because probates were not a standard practice and were considered "neither perfunctory nor conventional."[31] There are very strong variations in the probate items listed, the details of the inventories, and the depth of detail from one probate to the next. Because the conditions that led to recording a probate inventory were so disparate, none of the formulaic elements that ruled the recording of mortgage contracts appeared in the probate inventories. However, they are irreplaceable sources to reinforce the economic picture painted by the notarial contracts, and they supplement the standardized data with illustrative evidence of the pervasive uses of debt across sociodemographic strata in Yucatán. The probates used here cover a period of approximately fifty years, which while not exhaustive, is an acceptable sample for the summary uses with probates. Zephyr Frank, who wrote an excellent study of the Brazilian economy and wealth distribution in the entire nineteenth century, used approximately 659 probates.[32]

Book Outline

This book proceeds thematically rather than chronologically. The second chapter lays out Yucatán's regional and historical background, while exploring its postcolonial transition to a capitalist economy in laying the foundation for its emerging personal credit market. In the mid-nineteenth century, Yucatán was a heterogeneous region: urban and rural, native Maya and mestizo, rich and poor—all these elements collided and overlapped. The nineteenth century was also marked by the aftermath of a secession war, an ongoing civil conflict with ethnic overtones, and the agricultural henequen boom that exacerbated the region's economic disparities while increasingly tying it to the global market.

Chapter 3 focuses on the mortgages themselves and the development of the mortgage market in the wake of the 1857 Constitution and ensuing Reform Laws. The progressive bent of these laws, especially their reversal on the issue of the civil enforcement of usury laws, freed interest rates and opened the way for credit contracts to charge a price that reflected the risk each loan represented. This chapter addresses the importance and many interpretations of mortgages, not just as a documentary source in the book, but also as a critical interaction around which to analyze historical change in Mexico. Mortgages recorded by notaries are abundant in Latin American archives, and these debt contracts became the cornerstone of the credit market in Yucatán because of changes in the legal codes and the regional infrastructure. The contracts represent more than historical documents; they need to be understood and studied as an aggregate record of economic and social interactions in Yucatán.

The fourth chapter analyzes the formal and informal roles of notaries. The formal and explicit role was established by nineteenth-century laws and notarial codes. The informal role, developed as a result of the economic boom, highlighted the flexibility of the notary's inherent ability to act as an intermediary. This chapter further addresses the mechanisms by which notaries aided in the development of financial vehicles better suited to the new economic climate created by the henequen boom. Without banks, the shift from a subsistence economy to export-led growth relied on, among other things, reinterpretations of personal networks. Notaries were uniquely equipped to become intermediaries in transactions based on trust and the quality of the information on which loan agreements hinged. The chapter explains what notaries did and shows the mechanics of how a social network of hacienda owners and enterprising merchants, as well as members of the elite, financed a boom without banks. The analysis of notarial functions in Yucatán's mortgage market reveals notaries' contributions to the creation of this market. Their active participation in recording contracts and connecting clients demonstrates how, in the absence of banks, they facilitated access to credit and created networks of clients that strengthened the role of individual connections in the mortgage boom.

The importance and role of property rights in credit markets is the subject

of the fifth chapter. The progressive reforms of Mexico's liberal legal transformation in the nineteenth century significantly expanded property rights
and protection for its citizens, but it did not do this for all citizens equally.
Gender was the main factor for this legal iniquity, as women had incom-
plete property rights, with a corresponding effect on their diminished
status in Mexican society. The nineteenth century extended the legal
inferiority for women that had originated in the colonial legal codes.
Marriage still bound a wife to her husband in financial, physical, and
moral ways, and a mother could not be the guardian of her own children
if she was a widow. She could not enter into contracts on her own, she
had no official or public political power, and her legal and professional
roles were often in opposition or subservient to men. This legal inferiority was substantiated in the mortgage records, where the effect of property rights comes to light. While colonial records have long recorded the
financial activity of widows who acquired their husband's wealth after his
death and invested in local loans, the literature has never considered the
implications for female borrowers or the fact that married female borrowers generally paid much higher interest than their male counterparts.[33]
This chapter highlights how laws that were not created to address or respond to credit markets profoundly affected those who participated in
them. It also countervails the conventional wisdom about the position of
women in Latin American societies, in credit markets, and under the law
in this period.

Monopoly, rent-seeking behavior, and insider networks are the scourge
of developing economies, and in Mexico this trend toward small and concentrated economic activity has generally been observed among the powerful, the elite, and the government, which centralize their power and
ration access to the fruits of that power. Chapter 6 explores this tendency
within the notarial profession in Yucatán. Notaries were central to the
financial mechanics in Yucatán, but they can hardly be considered elite,
nor was their profession the nexus of power. Notaries were only one of the
many institutions of civil law and civil power, and yet the tendency toward
monopoly was reflected among them too. This chapter delves into this
drive toward monopoly through the case study of one of the most important notaries in Mérida and his entrepreneurial and monopolistic bent in
the mortgage market. This notary provides a prime example of the role of
personal connections in fostering personal success in Mexico. As this
chapter on Patrón Zavalegui's practice and business demonstrates, this
much-touted characteristic of Mexico's economic markets permeates all

levels of power and importance in society. As he became the engine of growth in the local credit market, he also became a monopolist among notaries. This combination of growth, entrepreneurship, and monopoly mirrors a pattern that is all too common in Yucatán and Mexico and reveals once more the mechanisms that have long operated there. Chapter 7 provides the conclusion.

Chapter Two

The Local Becomes Global

From Caste War to Henequen Boom

> Of all the bread-eating Americans, probably only a few have ever heard of
> henequen. Yet without henequen we could hardly harvest our grain crops,
> and consequently without henequen we could hardly get bread.
> —Gregory Mason, staff correspondent to *Outlook* in Mexico, 1916

The growth of Yucatán's economy and mortgage market did not happen
in a vacuum. The nineteenth-century transformation of Yucatán was
born out of local and global changes: the local adjustments to national
independence and the revolution in the global commodity markets. The
outcome in Yucatán of these twin developments was the growth of large-
scale export agriculture, expanded education and cultural venues, paved
and drained streets, hospitals, trains and trams, and an active, productive,
commercial economy connected to global markets. By the end of the
nineteenth century, Yucatán's achievements reflected the Mexican ideals
of a modern and progressive society that could compare itself favorably
with what it considered its European counterparts.

Yucatán had indeed come very far, transforming itself from a small,
inward-looking, subsistence economy into an export-oriented plantation
economy with global connections. It was not a commercially relevant
province of the colonial Spanish Empire, but by the end of the nineteenth
century, it was one of the fastest growing economies in Mexico. It collected enough local tax income to finance the infrastructure developments
that made it so modern, and it was connected by a combination of naval
and railroad routes to important trading centers in Havana, Louisiana,
New York, and Mexico City.

As would be expected, the transformation in Yucatán's local economy
was accompanied by a growing demand for credit, which happened mostly

in the private mortgage market. In 1895 notaries recorded almost nine hundred thousand pesos in mortgage loans in Mérida compared to the nearly six hundred thousand of outstanding mortgages of the two Yucatecan banks that year (see table 2.1). The nine hundred thousand pesos in mortgages that the notaries recorded were roughly equivalent at the time to seven hundred thousand U.S. dollars, an amount that understates the real value of the notarial credit contracts because it does not account for the maturity of the loans. The maturity of mortgage loans in notarial contracts was on average between two and ten years. The standard length of a bank loan in the 1890s, on the other hand, was six months. Together, the two Yucatecan banks held nearly six hundred thousand pesos in outstanding long-term loans in 1895, with the bulk of their lending going to short-term trade credit and commercial paper. Notaries did not deal in this sort of short-term credit. Taking this into consideration, table 2.1 illustrates the rise in the amount of credit lent through the offices of the Mérida notaries—a likely response to the growth in the henequen economy. Mérida had approximately 50,000 inhabitants at the end of the century, and the entire northwest region of the state accounted for about 120,000; at best, 1 in 1,000 Yucatecans were borrowing at the end of the century—in this case, a consequence of the socioeconomic inequality in the region.

Even though few studies exist to which we can compare this market and the city in which it existed, there are two main reasons why this particular mortgage market would be small. The first reason is that mortgages are long-term loans, and even in the most overheated of economies, most borrowers rarely need (or can) borrow long-term more than a few times in

Table 2.1   Loans through notaries and banks, Mérida (pesos)

	Mortgages through notaries	Mortgages through banks	Other loans through banks
1850	74,159 (68)	—	—
1860	84,004 (68)	—	—
1870	126,211 (133)	—	—
1875	157,787 (58)	—	—
1880	268,752 (102)	—	—
1885	130,077 (61)	—	—
1890	907,054 (129)	199,120	1,051,709
1895	892,051 (111)	591,327	2,389,469

Source: Protocolos notariales, AGEY and ANEY; "Balance promedio de bancos."

Note: The number of contracts in notarial records are shown in parentheses.

their life.[1] Second, the size of the Yucatán population does not accurately reflect the extent of the potential credit market. The rest of this chapter addresses how demographic changes, civil unrest, and ethnic scissions interacted with the growth of the local henequen industry to determine the size and scope of the local mortgage market.

Demographic Shifts

Well before the Spanish conquered Yucatán in the sixteenth century and before henequen became Yucatán's main export crop, native Maya agriculture included maize, beans, squash, and various tropical fruits. Yucatecan agriculture continued to include these commodities during the colonial period, but Spanish concerns with the development of some form of cash crop led them to introduce livestock to the area. The colonial economic focus had always been silver mining, and Yucatán never attracted much attention for this purpose.[2] Instead, cattle became a feature of the dry limestone fields of the flat peninsula, which provided little water and absolutely no mining prospects.[3] The central region of Yucatán also produced sugar, but this commodity reached only a modicum of success in the late colonial period, and it could never compare to the levels seen in the neighboring island of Cuba.[4] Beyond small sugar plantations, Yucatán had a thriving local beekeeping and honey production industry in the early colonial period, and some haciendas in Yucatán had also produced tobacco for commercial sale. Small-scale manufacturing processors of soap and candle wax dotted the peninsula, but Yucatán's commercial endeavors before the mid-nineteenth century were modest and mostly aimed at the local market.[5] The arid limestone soil and poor irrigation networks constituted a significant obstacle to traditional large-scale agriculture of wheat or barley, limiting the scope of Yucatán's commercial reach in the colony and making it even less attractive to the Spanish Crown. Throughout the colonial period and until the mid-nineteenth century, Yucatán's economy remained small, regional, and insular. The exponential increase in the production and export of henequen in the nineteenth century expanded cultivated areas in the state and erased the last vestiges of the small colonial industries.

The agricultural transformation of the state had a demographic corollary, although accurate population figures for this period in Yucatán's history are difficult to pin down, partly because of this radical transformation.

Not only does the demographic effect of wars and plagues inject tremendous variability in the figures, but population censuses were not standardized or performed in a reliable manner until 1895. Complaints that the population censuses of the late 1860s were underreported were common among the different state municipalities.[6] Such complaints were not unfounded, because the census procedure required a registration process at which many people balked, leading many of the published figures on population before 1895 to probably have a downward bias. Furthermore, the comparisons between years are complicated by the fact that the limits of the towns changed from census to census. The area of Mérida sometimes included surrounding towns whose geographical definitions were also continually redrawn for census purposes; other times the accounts for Mérida were limited to the city; still other times they included the whole region. Even if we take some errors in census techniques into account, the Caste War casualties and the 1850s cholera epidemic produced a very steep decline in the population; tables 2.2a and 2.2b sketch the demographic effect of these nineteenth-century shocks.[7] The Caste War and plagues affected Mérida and the Northwest less, as it lost fewer inhabitants than the rest of the state during the times of unrest. Other parts of the state recovered in the aftermath of the worst fighting, but none managed to overtake the Northwest after the Caste War.

Table 2.2a   Population figures, Yucatán

	1845	1862	1883	1900
Northwest (includes Mérida)	92,194	82,881	113,841	129,994
Center	104,926	75,990	84,951	81,099
South	127,815	52,073	41,861	55,450
East	97,468	35,469	36,172	44,403
Total	422,403	246,413	276,825	310,946

SOURCE: Suárez Molina, *Evolución económica*.

Table 2.2b   Change in population (%)

	1845–62	1862–83	1883–1900	1845–1900
Northwest (includes Mérida)	− 10.10	37.35	14.19	41.00
Center	− 27.58	11.79	− 4.53	− 22.71
South	− 59.26	− 19.61	32.46	− 56.62
East	− 63.61	1.98	22.76	− 54.44
Total	− 41.66	12.34	12.33	− 26.39

SOURCE: Suárez Molina, *Evolución económica*.

The southern and eastern regions were most affected by population loss between 1845 and 1862, where most of the Caste War confrontations took place and where minor conflicts continued until the end of the century. These areas are also where population levels did not recover from earlier losses. The cholera epidemics were similarly most destructive here, although the plague struck pretty much throughout Yucatán in the 1850s. Diseases and war caused much of the population loss, which was only compounded by internal migration relocating in and around Mérida from the center, south, and east. Other people simply left the state. Starting in the 1860s, the 37 percent increase in population in the Northwest was the product of immigration from outlying areas, from other states in Mexico, and from abroad. Most foreign immigrants came from Spain, Great Britain, Cuba, Turkey, and China, and together with the Yucatecan internal migration, they contributed to the northwestern region's demographic recovery between 1862 and 1883.[8] Immigrants flocked to Yucatán's northwestern region because by then it was the center of economic activity. The population (local and immigrant) concentrated in the region around Mérida and along the railroads leading to the ports north of Mérida, and the demographic explosion of the Northwest skewed the population distribution in the aftermath of the Caste War and the henequen boom. Like out-of-state immigrants, most of the Yucatecan population lived in the henequen-producing Northwest, where the nonindigenous Yucatecans were the majority. Mérida and its northwestern port of Progreso were the two areas in which the population was mostly nonindigenous. In the rest of the state, indigenous Mayas generally continued to be a demographic majority, as illustrated in fig. 2.1.

The settlement of nonindigenous and indigenous Yucatecans in the henequen-producing areas during the boom is an expected outcome of the growth of the henequen economy. The causal relationship that has been drawn between the demographic shifts caused by the Caste War (see tables 2.2a and 2.2b) and the growth in this part of the state provide a compelling case study of ethnic rebellion and the ravages of export-led growth and concentration of wealth.[9] But reducing Yucatán's nineteenth-century history to that of secession and civil wars followed by the monopolistic trends and social consequences of the agricultural boom overstates the impact of one event (the war) and understates the effects of the structural shifts in the global economy and of technological innovation (the invention of the McCormick reaper and the demand for henequen from the United States)

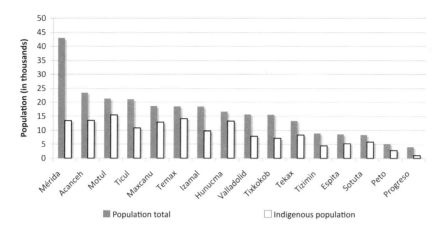

Fig. 2.1   Distribution of ethnic population, 1881
SOURCE: Rodríguez Losa, *Geografía política de Yucatán*.

that supported both the population growth in the area and the demo-graphic distribution throughout the state.

Structural Shocks

As the Caste War violence abated in the Northwest and moved out of the henequen zone into the less populated East and after the cholera breakout of 1853, Mexico and Yucatán were soon faced with upheavals caused by the continuing and escalating conflict between conservatives and liberals on the national stage. This conflict culminated in a new constitution in 1857, a bloody civil war between 1858 and 1861, and, finally, the 1861 invasion by European powers demanding repayment for Mexico's debts. It would take three years and the withdrawal of the Spanish and English troops, but when the Yucatecan military commander Felipe Navarrete met up with the French invasion force and accepted the French monarch Maximilian as emperor of Mexico in Yucatán in 1864, Navarrete was accepting peace in Yucatán after almost twenty-five years of unrest. Lay-ing down arms before the French occupation in 1864 also meant that for the first time in a very long time Yucatán could have focused on some-thing else besides political conflict. Unfortunately, this was not how it turned out.

Yucatán was traditionally poised to oppose any ruler it considered foreign, and the definition of foreign in Yucatán extended to anyone not from the peninsula. The state's secession bid in 1844 had been as much a reaction to centralist forces as a conviction that being beholden to the Mexican capital was equal to being beholden to a foreign nation. Twenty years after the secession bid, the Yucatán elite would not be very impressed with the willingness of Mexican conservatives to offer the Crown and Mexico to Maximilian of Habsburg. The political division between conservatives and liberals in Yucatán followed the national ones, with the two groups in similar straits, but Yucatecan regional identity trumped politics. After Navarrete's peace agreement, Yucatán was still reluctant to accept a foreign-born emperor's rule over the state. In a bid to ease tension in what was considered a remote part of the Mexican Empire, Empress Carlotta, Maximilian's wife, visited Yucatán in 1866, where "her charm disarmed the critics of foreign rule."[10] And although that may have been true, Benito Juárez's return to the helm of the national government flamed the tensions between conservatives and liberals in Yucatán when he restored the republic after executing Maximilian in 1867.

The restoration of the republic brought a new liberal governor to Yucatán: Manuel Cepeda Peraza, who defeated the conservative General Francisco Cantón on June 15, 1867. By December the conservative forces rebelled again, and Cantón became military commander and interim governor of Yucatán. Between December 1867 and January 1869, the revolving door of governors would swing twice in Yucatán, with reinforcements sent by Juárez to reclaim the governorship in the name of the liberals, while conservatives were laying siege to Mérida for two months. These power grabs had nothing to do with Maximilian or the monarchy; they were a continuation of the caudillo politics of the postindependence era in Mexico.

It wasn't until 1876, when Porfirio Díaz garnered power and legitimacy from both camps on the national scene, that the conflict between liberals and conservatives ceased to be the excuse or reason for the serial uprisings in Yucatán and elsewhere in the nation. Díaz had been a loyal supporter of Juárez during the French intervention, but he was also a critic of the Juárez government and Sebastián Lerdo de Tejada, the successor after Juárez's death in 1872. This position made it easier for Díaz to secure support from the two traditional opposing political factions. In 1874 Díaz was elected to Congress in Veracruz, and in November 1876 he became president and remained in that position until 1910. This period of relative calm would also be the period of Yucatán's henequen boom.

Yucatán, like much of Latin America, experienced significant economic growth between 1870 and 1930, largely based on exports of a primary good. This growth was bolstered by a series of government-sponsored protective mechanisms, which were not the result of a political commitment to infant industry protection or a prestructuralist challenge to free trade, but instead a reflection of the inequality in the societies in which this growth was taking place.[11] In Yucatán nothing could have predicted the revolution in American farming that led to the henequen boom. The development of mechanical binders that reaped and tied bundles of grain mechanically in the United States would change the yields of American agriculture forever. More important, since the McCormick mechanical binder and reaper used Yucatecan twine to bind the grains it harvested, the transformation in American agriculture also radically altered the Yucatecan economic structure. As Juárez, Maximilian, and Díaz traded places at the helm of Mexico's leadership, Yucatán became an agricultural export-based colossus because of the McCormick mechanical reaper and the state's almost exclusive global supply of henequen, the reaper and binder's ideal fiber. In fact, the invention of the machine in 1878 might have been enough to sustain a rise in Yucatán's export of henequen, because the hard, binding fiber had no competitors until very late in the century. In addition to the McCormick reaper and a plentiful henequen supply, two other factors expanded henequen exports: (1) the economic policy of President Porfirio Díaz rewarded industrial innovation and export production with political favors, and (2) the gradual depreciation of silver to gold as of 1870 made—for a country such as Mexico that remained on a de facto silver standard—export prices increasingly attractive to a gold-standard country like the United States.

Earlier in the century, planters had enjoyed henequen profits from the sale of the fiber for naval cordage to European and American ports. Yucatán faced stiff competition in the naval cordage industry from other producers such as Russia and the Philippines, and in 1878 Juan Miguel Castro went to Europe as an envoy of the state governor, Amador Barbachano, to market Yucatecan henequen to European ports. In a state-sponsored bid to expand Yucatán's consumer base beyond the United States, he hoped to wrestle out from under the stranglehold of the henequen-trading companies. By 1874 henequen already accounted for 74 percent of export revenues, three-quarters of which were sold to U.S. cordage companies through the trading companies of Escalante and Dondé.[12] The European marketing trip on the eve of the McCormick binder's invention also reveals the region's concerns with its position in the world economy. Yucatán wanted to expand its market, but it was also keenly aware of the difficulty of supplying a distant European market. Supply and quality were of main concern to the European shipping ports, which told Castro (as he wrote in his report) that they were concerned Yucatán would not be able to produce enough fiber for their needs.[13] They need not have worried about the volume of henequen Yucatán was capable of producing.

The invention of the McCormick mechanical binder led to a surge in U.S. demand for henequen from Yucatán, which more than satisfied this demand and gave up all thoughts of diversifying beyond the United States. The balance between weight and strength provided by henequen (as compared with other binding fibers), combined with Yucatán's proximity to the American agricultural markets that used the mechanical binder, committed Yucatán to the U.S. market and set off the henequen boom.[14]

Fig. 2.2 traces the increasing production of henequen and the rising export income it generated during the last quarter of the nineteenth century. Production in tons nearly quadrupled over the first ten years between

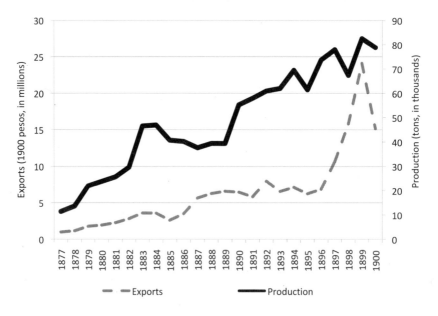

Fig. 2.2   Henequen exports and production
SOURCE: *Estadísticas económicas.*

1877 and 1887 and more than doubled again between 1887 and 1897. As points of reference, the McCormick mechanical binder was introduced in 1878, and the first banks opened in Yucatán in 1899.

Henequen Production

Work on a henequen plantation was arduous and time sensitive. Peasants and day laborers harvested the henequen leaves by hacking them off the base of the plant with a machete. These leaves were then loaded onto a manual wheelbarrow or a wheeled platform pulled by a donkey to the main plantation house. Plantation owners lay narrow-gauge, Decauville rails throughout their plantation as quickly as they could get the rails, and soon donkeys efficiently pulled the henequen-laden platform wagons on the rails to the main hacienda, where the fiber was quickly extracted from the leaves and then hung to dry.

Yucatecan henequen was especially labor intensive because it was harvested year-round. Philippine abaca fiber, henequen's main competitor, was constrained by more rigorous seasonal harvesting schedules. Even if heavy rains in the summer complicated both the harvesting and drying process, in Yucatán plantation workers harvested most of the year. They assessed when each henequen leaf reached peak fiber strength and cut it off the main plant. The leaf remained at its peak strength for a few weeks while it was on the plant, but once it had been cut off the plant, the window between harvest and fiber extraction was about twenty-four hours long, after which the fiber dried inside the leaf and became impossible to extract.[15]

Plantation workers harvested the leaves manually because not all *pencas* (the large pointy leaves of the agave) on a plant were ready to be harvested at the same time. Early in the nineteenth century the fiber was also manually combed out of the plant. Metal combs scratched and rasped at the flesh of the plant to string out the pulp and the fiber, which was then hung out to dry in the sun along wooden racks specially built for this purpose. The local government promoted innovation to develop better rasping techniques by running competitions, and the first machine to successfully do this was the Solís machine, a basic henequen rasper, powered by horses or humans.[16] During the course of the boom, technological innovation and the use of iron instead of wood helped streamline the machine, and the adoption of steam power significantly increased the speed at which fiber was extracted from the henequen leaf. The engines that powered the machines were imported from the United States, Canada, and Great Britain, and the rasping machine, itself a local invention, was also produced abroad. Once a mold for the machine had been designed in Yucatán, it was sent to overseas foundries and machine-building shops.[17]

Independent farmers with only a few henequen plants on their plots did not own rasping machines and sold their leaves to the larger haciendas with machinery, which then processed and sold the henequen fiber to the trading houses in Mérida. As soon as the fiber was dry, it was rolled into bales and first transported to the ports of Sisal and Progreso, then exported to the United States, where it was manufactured into ropes and binding twine. The local industry never successfully developed rope factories because the emphasis in the trade finance remained on the raw product, where the highest added value lay.

Production of henequen increased more than tenfold between 1877 and 1900, and 97 percent of this production was exported.[18] A few large, locally owned trading houses managed the trade of henequen, which increased from six thousand tons in 1875 to nearly eighty thousand tons in 1900.[19] The plantations sold their henequen to the trading houses, and they in turn exported it. These trading houses advanced credit to henequen planters before the creation of the Yucatecan banks in the 1890s. In the absence of formal banking institutions, their business with U.S. trading houses such as Thebaud Brothers and Peabody and Company gave them access to credit, which they used to finance the plantations. By the late nineteenth century, three trading houses had cornered the henequen trading market, and by 1903 International Harvester Company, acting through Peabody and the Molina trading house, had become the region's primary purchaser of henequen.

Transformation to Capitalism

During the henequen boom, technological innovation overlapped with investment in transportation. The first types of railroads in Yucatán were narrow-gauge rail lines that provided easier transport from the fields to the rasping machines within the plantations. This initial development was followed by the installation of normal-gauge trains that connected the plantations to the port of Sisal and later to the port of Progreso, from where the fiber was exported. Henequen was the main cargo of these railroads, but they also carried other goods shipped out of or into Yucatán through Sisal and Progreso. Trains also carried passengers, and ticket sales on the railroads increased throughout the end of the nineteenth century from approximately 25,000 tickets sold in 1880 to 250,000 tickets in 1900.[20]

Mérida transformed along with Yucatán, changing from a provincial town into a cosmopolitan center. Fortunes grew, and the lasting influence of Maximilian's court, which had sanctioned Europhile tendencies of the aspirational Mexican consumer, was emulated by Porfirio Díaz. Goods from Spain had been status purchases during the colonial period and the trend regained strength in the nineteenth century. The revival was not solely based on consumer goods, although these certainly were imported en masse. As the probate inventory of a Mérida pharmacist who died in 1874 shows, his pharmacy included sassafras from Bristol and English calcinate magnesium, as well as candles and mints from Vichy and Reynauld, France. At home, he also had a French-Spanish/Spanish-French dictionary, a few French grammar books, and a Spanish translation of William H. Prescott's 1837 *The History of the Reign of Ferdinand and Isabella*.[21] The material aspirations were matched by the cultural investments that the Mérida society prized, and support for the arts and leisure entertainment became a fixture of the city.[22]

Thorstein Veblen never traveled to Yucatán, but his descriptions of conspicuous consumption among the leisure class overlap with many of the transgressions of which Yucatán's elites have been accused.[23] The aspirational tendencies that were given license under Maximilian's empire were further supported by the income generated by exports of henequen during the rest of the century. The grand Belle Époque homes that were built at the turn of the century along Mérida's elegant Paseo Montejo contrasted sharply with the standard of living of peasants and Maya plantation workers who made this lifestyle possible. The sins of which the henequen boom has been accused were perhaps not so much due to the conspicuous wealth of the few, but the enormous disparity between the wealth of the few and the poverty of the many. In the henequen zone, which spread in a radius of about eighty kilometers (fifty miles) around Mérida, villagers were drawn into a tight-knit circle with planters, traders, and urban dwellers, and the inequalities inherent in the system were obvious to anyone.[24]

The indigenous population of Yucatán provided the labor for this capitalistic economic transition. Much as indigenous labor oiled the wheels of colonial industries and trade, so did it also in Yucatán during the nineteenth century. The indigenous population benefited only marginally from this transition, and long-standing patterns of economic participation and wealth distribution were replicated. From the perspective of the rest of the nonindigenous middle-class and elite inhabitants of Mérida, henequen ushered in modernity. The boom made wage-earners of peasants and millionaires out of hacienda owners, while turning the provincial backwater into an international trading partner. Local population movements supported this transition, relocating the workforce where it would be most needed when the demands for Yucatecan binding twine exploded. The growth of the credit market was a corollary of this transformation, as was its complete lack of Maya participants. There would not have been a henequen boom without Maya workers, but there would be a credit market without them.

Henequen was the engine that propelled Yucatán's transition to capitalism. It was the reason railroads crisscrossed its plantations and connected them to key ports. It altered the physical layout of the region and thrust Yucatán into a modern capitalist age, complete with the inequities that are part of a rapidly transforming economy.

Ethnicity, Inequality, and Local Markets

The size of the growing Yucatán credit market was at odds with the size of its population, and this can be understood only as a reflection of Yucatán's fractured society. The henequen boom affected the growth of private credit in the notarial offices, but it could not overcome the ethnic scission in its society. The inequality between indigenous Maya inhabitants and nonindigenous people of the peninsula was not a consequence of the henequen boom. It had originated in the colonial economy and continued well into the nineteenth century, and the mortgage market makes that painfully obvious. The private mortgage market did not include one single loan made by or to a Maya. The history of the Yucatecan mortgage market does not include Mayas, who overwhelmingly (but not exclusively) represented the poorest members of Yucatán's society; the history cannot be understood without paying attention to this exclusion—it is a powerful reminder of the effect of poverty and inequality on the development of financial markets.

The dearth of Maya participants in the Yucatán credit market was accompanied by a very high degree of inequality between Maya and non-

Maya peoples. Yucatán's indigenous Maya did not incorporate into Spanish colonial society as other indigenous people did in the Mexican highlands, where high levels of intermarriage quickly complicated the ethnic composition of the population. The lack of colonial interregional trading and mining routes through Yucatán limited this trend. Yucatán's main contribution to the colonial structure instead was as the regional bishopric, which asserted the colonial power and control of the Spanish ecclesiastical arm in this remote recess of New Spain. Yucatán's archbishopric had jurisdiction over the states of Yucatán, Tabasco, and Campeche, and from Mérida it managed the spiritual conquest of the church over the Maya people.[25] When Mexico became independent from Spain, regional power struggles erupted throughout the country, including Yucatán. The 1844 secession bid was one of these struggles, and its resolution in Yucatán upset a precarious balance between the Maya population and the availability of arable land.

Yucatán's uneasy relationship with the Mexican Republic it had decided to join in 1823 led to a costly and unsuccessful secession bid in 1839. The survival of the Mexican union was paramount for the Mexican government at that moment. President Santa Anna (who infamously charged the Alamo) ordered the Mexican army to blockade the Yucatecan ports and force the separatists to remain in the union. The national and military pressure pushed Yucatán to relinquish—and the union survived. But the protracted internal debates over state rights versus federal rights that led to the secession bid in the first place had also destabilized some of the guarantees that Maya villages had enjoyed during the colonial period. The failed autonomy of the Yucatecan state provoked questions about the autonomy of the indigenous villages, and as the state debated its limited autonomy, it started to question the autonomy of the Maya villages.[26]

The high costs of keeping an army and defending itself against the blockade had led the state to resort to the time-tested practice of granting ownership of uncultivated and unclaimed lands as payment to soldiers. These baldío (uncultivated) lands were often on the outskirts of villages and were considered community property by the villagers, who always left some plots fallow. The baldío land was therefore neither unclaimed nor uncultivated in the eyes of the villagers. Coupled with the failed promise by the Yucatán government to respect the legal transfer of land from colonial haciendas to independent villages, rural unrest concerning the land promises escalated into what has since become known as the Caste War.[27] The ethnic overtones of the Caste War were rooted in the unequal distribution of land as repayment to soldiers, made worse by the confiscation of lands to make these payments.[28]

The Caste War was not the first rural rebellion in Mexico, nor was it the first strife in Yucatán that amalgamated ethnic and peasant dissatisfactions, but it was unprecedented in its strategic organization, violence, and historical portent and legacy.[29] Jacinto Canek, who still remains a hero in the mind of the Maya and Yucatecans, led a rebellion in 1761 that lasted only one month, but his was the name invoked when the Caste War broke out in 1847.[30] This time, the turmoil would last much longer, altering the state's demographic composition, as people moved out of the regions where the rebellions raged most violently between 1849 and 1851 and settled in and around relatively peaceful Mérida, where the henequen plantations promised employment. Nelson Reed, chronicler of the Caste War, describes in detail how the war pitted Maya and mestizo civilians and soldiers against mainly white landowners, but also against other Maya and mestizo bystanders to the conflict.[31] Scholarly analyses that point to the political, economic, and social aspects of the rebellion and the ethnic overtones in the conflict have supplemented his journalistic account.[32] Fleeing unrest as well as locust plagues, cholera epidemics, and famines, an increasing numbers of peasants, most of them Maya, moved to work on haciendas and in the cities.[33] The displacement caused by the Caste War provided a ready labor force for the incipient boom, itself a response to international demand for henequen. Between this local ethnic conflict and the inherent social conflicts that are created when economic growth is not spread evenly, lies the framework of the Yucatán credit market.

The privileges of non-Maya mestizo and whites over native Maya Yucatecans permeated all levels of social interaction, and the historical records provide many examples of ethnic inequality during the nineteenth century. Table 2.3 quantifies the wealth distribution in Yucatán using 337 probate records of Mayas (identified by their last name) and non-Mayas (mestizo or foreign) who died in Yucatán and left an inventory of their estates.[34]

Probates were a notarial task, but unlike mortgage contracts, which needed to be recorded to be enforceable, probates were required only if the estate was large, if there were minors among the heirs, and if the estate was contested. If the estate was incontestably divided through a will or if the decedent was too poor, there would be no probate, so the amounts listed in table 2.3 most likely overestimate the wealth of the Yucatán population, because they cannot account for deaths that did not produce a

Table 2.3 Summary data of Maya and non-Maya probates

	Maya	Non-Maya
Typical occupation	Small landowner, land worker, menial laborer (and women)	Landowner, trader (and women)
Number of probates, 1847–70	28	40
Number of probates, 1871–1901	100	169
Total	128	209

SOURCE: Subserie testamentos, Fondo Justicia Civil, AGEY.

NOTE: The non-Maya category includes mestizo and foreign-born Europeans who became residents of Yucatán. The occupation of women in the probates always identified their domestic chores, and so instead of referring to these, I identified the women as such in the table.

probate. This omission affects the Maya population particularly because they are underrepresented in the probate records. But if the decedent left heirs who were minors, then a probate had to be drawn up, whether the estate had any assets or not. The majority of the probates in the archive are from non-Maya decedents, a likely reflection of the geographical bias of the data that privileged Mérida over other towns where more Mayas lived and an indication of the economic conditions under which Mayas died— they were less likely to leave large estates or be involved in large credit deals that would trigger a probate. That said, the amount of Maya probates is still significant and revealing—a not insignificant third of the probates are of Mayas, and not all of them are from impoverished decedents who died before their children reached adulthood. Taking all this into account, the probates are extremely useful. Table 2.3 illustrates the levels of inequality that existed in Yucatán during the nineteenth century and provides a powerful reason for the lack of Maya borrowers or lenders in the mortgage market. If nothing else, the table provides a powerful explanation for the size of Mérida's mortgage market—a large number of the population could simply not mortgage any property because they had none.

Table 2.4 summarizes some of the basic measures of inequality. There is a large difference between the average and the median net worth of the decedents, which is caused by the extreme figures in the series. For example, among non-Mayas, Roque Jacinto Campos died in 1889 with an estate valued at more than one million pesos. This amounts to 67 percent of the recorded wealth for the period. The median better reflects the average wealth held by the majority of people in the sample.

Table 2.4 Net worth distribution from probates, Yucatán, 1847–1901 (pesos)

Average net worth	15,512
(including zero assets)	(6,763)
Median net worth	1,153
(including zero assets)	(0)
Proportion of wealth held by richest man, including probates with zero assets	67.47%
Proportion of wealth held by people with above average net worth	89.77%

Source: Subserie testamentos, Fondo Justicia Civil, AGEY.

Note: Figures in parentheses reflect the average and median, inclusive of the sizable number of probates that stated zero wealth.

The inequality in wealth distribution in Yucatán had been a feature of the colonial period, and the henequen boom did not change that. If anything, economic growth exacerbated wealth disparities. Table 2.5 splits the probates into two periods roughly corresponding to the period preceding the boom and the period after the boom. This exercise makes the discrepancy and the effect of the boom even more obvious. As the table illustrates, the growth of the average wealth of Mayas over the two periods is dwarfed by the rise in the wealth of non-Mayas.

Table 2.5 Average wealth at time of probate (pesos)

Period of probate	Maya	Non-Maya
Preboom: 1847–70	602	9,343
Postboom: 1871–1901	1,280	35,317
Percentage increase between periods	212	378

Source: Subserie testamentos, Fondo Justicia Civil, AGEY.

Mayas who died before the boom died poorer than Mayas who died during the period of growth. This relative improvement in Maya wealth suggests that everyone benefited from the growth of the economy, but it is also an illustration of its cruel disparities. Non-Maya Yucatecans were the ones who really saw their fortunes multiply. They were better off than Mayas even before 1871, and if they survived into the henequen boom, their estate grew almost four times larger than the earlier period and almost thirty times larger than a Maya's estate. These aggregated results reinforce what has often been said about the henequen boom: it disproportionately benefited those who were already better off.

This discrepancy is a powerful explanation as to why Mérida's mortgage market served only non–Maya lenders and borrowers. A significant portion of the population of Yucatán did not have the capital to build and benefit from the boom or even borrow to participate. It is an almost undisputed fact that well-functioning credit markets help and support economic development, but as the Yucatán case exemplifies, heterogeneity in society is replicated in the markets.

Chapter Three

Usury, Ethnicity, and the Market
National Laws and Local Effects

In all the laws of the Republic, the usury prohibitions are
forthwith abolished. In consequence, the rate and interest is now
up to the decision of the concerned parties.
—Benito Juárez, 1861

Credit is a ubiquitous feature of society, which regulated it and developed
social mores to manage it well before banks and bank charters and banking
regulations. In fact, usury laws are historically some of the oldest credit
regulations used to control the flow and the price of credit. This chapter
focuses on the conditions and circumstances under which credit existed
and grew in Yucatán before the creation of banks. I highlight mid-nine-
teenth-century legislation that contributed to the formation and growth
of a personal mortgage market prior to banks and chart the creation of
a mortgage market more precisely. Thus, credit was formal, responded to
incentives, and grew to support the economy. Nonbank credit generated
economic growth and the creation of banks—and in Yucatán we can observe the development of a market through the mortgages and credit that
were not tied to what the literature has often considered a sine qua non—
economic growth needs credit, but it does not need banks.

When two banks opened in Mérida to help finance the growing trade
of henequen in 1889, they successfully added liquidity to a cash-poor
economy and raised equity for a developing infrastructure. Both the Banco
Mercantil de Yucatán and the Banco Yucateco became the significant financial backers of the henequen industry at the very end of the century,
but not before mortgages had become the most important source of long-
term credit in the region.[1] The private mortgage market continued to

thrive because of the restraints that were imposed on the newly chartered banks. Banks could not lend for longer than six months and special mortgage banks were not created until the very end of the century.

National Changes

Liberal emphasis on the separation of church and state in the mid-nineteenth century caused one of the most significant rifts in postindependence Mexican society. Not until the Mexican Revolution in the early twentieth century would the country once again be as divided as it was in the 1850s and 1860s. Throughout the republic, liberals and conservatives primarily debated and fought over the controversial issue of states' rights and independence. The debate over the relationship between church and state, a conflict that crossed state lines and encompassed the entire country in a wave of conflicting political loyalties, was no less divisive. The privatization of communal and ecclesiastical land, enacted by the politically liberal factions in the new constitution of 1857, provoked violent dissent and led to almost four years of war. This rash of civil confrontations would become the Reform War, and it raged between conservatives and liberals until 1861, when Benito Juárez ultimately gained control. The result was a new legal code, the Código de la Reforma, that reinforced and expanded the 1857 Constitution. The code removed the church from most civil interactions, dispossessed it of most of its landed property, and initiated the privatization of ecclesiastical and communal lands. The church held considerable wealth, but the loss and privatization of the village commons (*ejidos*) would affect a larger number of people. The changes to communal property were so profound, widespread, and radical that the abolition of usury restraints, which was included in the 1861 changes, received relatively little attention.

Usury controls in the Mexican civil laws had been directly related to ecclesiastical edicts on the evils of profiting from other people's suffering. These controls were not specific to Mexico, as most of the Catholic world was subject to them.[2] Catholics were not alone in scorning interest rates; in the Muslim world, for example, an intricate system of interest-free banking had developed over centuries to counteract the absolute prohibition of interest rates. In this interest-free world, the costs and risks associated with credit were translated into legal fees or transactions costs, circumventing the laws that forbade interest but charging a price nevertheless.

In Catholic Mexico, interest rates were not forbidden, but the price of credit was regulated and fixed and had been so for decades.[3] In many crucial ways the credit market was hampered and constrained in similar ways as if interest rates had been forbidden altogether. Interest rates could not exceed 5 percent for personal loans and 6 percent for commercial loans, and anything above these charges was considered usurious and illegal.

As leader of the liberal party and president of Mexico, Benito Juárez lifted usury restrictions at the end of the Reform War, when his victory over conservative forces gave him the political capital with which to impose sweeping reforms. These liberal reforms were embodied in the 1857 Constitution and launched the Reform War, the end of which provided the opportunity to end the ban of usury in 1861—a ban that was considered outdated and contrary to the progressive tone and zeitgeist of a liberal republic. In March 1861, following the expulsion from Mexico of the apostolic delegate of the Vatican in January and its five bishops a few days later, Juárez officially decreed what is perhaps one of the most overlooked pieces of reform legislation: on March 15 he repealed the usury laws, thereby eliminating the legal enforcement of usury limits. He went on to address the antiquated and illiberal practice of hemming in an "individual's right to set interest rates at whichever level he wished" and made it illegal to curb the free establishment of interest rates. Nary an eyebrow was lifted in Mérida or anywhere else at Juárez's pronouncements against these ecclesiastical bans and his support of the freedoms of commerce.[4] It was, however, a momentous decree, and one that would be largely responsible for a radical change in the credit market. The 1861 decree was formally codified in the 1870 Civil Code.[5]

The Juárez victory celebrations were short-lived, as both sides in the Reform War had incurred significant debts to European lending nations, and in 1861 Juárez declared a two-year moratorium on debt repayments. Mexico owed Spain, England, and France, and now that the war was over, they expected repayment. In November 1861 Spanish troops seized the port of Veracruz, with British and French fleets soon following. Spain and England were mostly interested in establishing a presence to convince Mexico to repay (and to show Spanish and British creditors that their government was acting on their behalf). France, on the other hand, had grander designs. The invasion would allow Napoleon III to establish a tentative stronghold in a part of the world he intended to use to extend the reach of France's power.[6]

Conservatives welcomed the invasion because it also completely destabilized the precarious homegrown liberal project they despised. They saw
the invasion as an opportunity to regain the political high ground they
had lost in 1861. Monarchical rule, even by a foreign monarch, was not an
impossible concept in Mexico. The idea had been bandied about as a potential political system after Mexico claimed independence from Spain in
1821—and named Agustín de Iturbide emperor and first ruler.[7] With the
Mexican treasury depleted and foreign forces on Mexican soil, the possibility of installing a foreign monarch provided Mexican conservatives
with a solution. By 1863 the French army had weakened Juárez's forces
and marched on Puebla and Mexico City, victorious and cheered on by
supporters of the conservative camp. Juárez withdrew north and Napoleon's Austrian cousin, archduke Maximilian of Habsburg, became Mexico's second emperor.

Maximilian of Habsburg did not do as his conservative supporters in
Mexico expected. He did not restore clerical power or corporatist traditions, which he considered archaic. Maximilian's vision as the imported
and enlightened ruler of Mexico was to bring modernity to an underde-
veloped land, much as Juárez had, in fact, intended. During Maximilian's
short reign, Mexico's institutional framework was bolstered by the 1865
Civil Code, which included (1) guarantees to individual property rights,
especially to the purchasers of church property; (2) the first commercial
code; and (3) a notarial code—all fashioned after French examples. Under
Maximilian, the first comprehensive postcolonial notarial code, the Ley
Orgánica del Notariado y del Oficio de Escribano, established clear rules
for the notary's function and made the rules applicable throughout the
entire nation.

To great conservative disappointment, Maximilian did not overturn
the liberal bent of Mexico's legal regime promulgated under Juárez. He
did not alter the intent of the Reform Laws, nor did he revoke the anti-
clerical laws; in fact, he reaffirmed the sale of church property and the
liberty of worship in 1865. He also used his position as the European head
of state of a Latin American country to create incentives for international
trade. Under Maximilian, French capital revitalized the textile industry,
and British investment continued work on railroad lines connecting Mexico City to the port of Veracruz, encouraging European immigration to
Mexico.[8] The liberal ethos that Juárez had painstakingly introduced with
his reforms would become dominant after the restoration of the Mexican
Republic, and this was in many ways also a consequence of Maximilian,

who not only maintained the liberal maxims introduced by Juárez but enshrined them into codes and laws.

The greatest testament to the liberal nature of Maximilian's rule was that Juárez did not overturn most of Maximilian's legal codes when he restored the republic in 1867. As soon as Juárez returned to power after the French had withdrawn and Maximilian had been executed, he not only reinstated the Reform Laws as such, including those abrogating usury restrictions, but also kept the civil, commercial, and notarial codes enacted under Maximilian. The 1870 Civil Code was, in fact, a hastily republicanized version of the civil code enacted by Maximilian in 1865.

Usury and the Mortgage Market

In colonial Mexico, the church had been one of the most important lenders, providing a significant proportion of capital to colonial merchants and trade.[9] This changed in the nineteenth century, which was not kind to the church in Mexico. The first blow came in 1805 when, in the context of the Bourbon reforms, the Spanish Crown sequestered many ecclesiastical funds. This process, the Consolidación de Vales Reales, required loans made by ecclesiastical funds to miners, merchants, traders, and any other of the church's debtors to be paid to the Crown over the following ten years.[10]

The second blow was the liberal attack on church and communal wealth and privileges in the middle of the nineteenth century. This attack was part of the conflict between liberal and conservative Mexicans, which, starting in 1857, gradually dispossessed the church of all its wealth, as well as its legal hold on the practice of credit. Benito Juárez's decree abolishing usury restrictions in 1861 not only liberalized the price of credit but legislated the banishment of the church in the credit market. When Juárez abolished usury and all constraints on the price of credit on March 15, 1861, he eliminated the concept of unjustified gain, which was one of the philosophical definitions of usury. In the modern Mexico Juárez fashioned, the notion that pecuniary gain implied guilt was a throwback to a colonial, premodern Mexico, and his decree effectively ushered in a new chapter in Mexico's financial history.

As the church's deep involvement in credit markets in the colonial period attests, the existence of usury laws did not eliminate money lending. On the contrary, usury laws existed because of the ubiquity of credit, because merchant and trade credits were essential to the development of colonial markets.[11] In the absence of banks and with the disappearance of ecclesiastical lending, mortgages and personal loans would become even more important in nineteenth-century Yucatán. The controls on usury were lifted in the 1860s, and economic growth fueled by demand for locally grown henequen stimulated the demand for credit and the growth of a credit market. Foreign brokers were active in the later part of the century, when foreign demand for henequen made it lucrative to invest in Yucatán, but before the henequen boom, Yucatán borrowers could not rely on any institutional forms of credit. On the eve of the henequen boom, credit was private and informal. Personal loans were common, as probate records reveal, but the bulk of recorded and collateralized credit was in mortgages, which were recorded by notaries. By definition, notaries were central to the credit process because only they were allowed to record mortgage contracts, giving the contracts legal weight and enforceability.

The End of Usury

Until 1861 the legal interest rate of noncommercial loans was capped at 5 percent, while commercial loans could charge 6 percent per year. Most interest-bearing loans in the nineteenth-century records did, in fact, charge 6 percent interest per year.[12] Interest-rate ceilings were upheld in the civil laws until the 1857 Constitution and consequent Reforms Laws. The 1857 Constitution and decrees stemming from the liberal push to exclude the church from political and economic interaction put an end to formal usury bans, and interest rates quickly rose above the outdated 6 percent ecclesiastical limit.[13]

Historians have long recognized that thin capital markets and inefficient credit institutions were obstacles to economic growth in nineteenth-century Mexico.[14] Usury laws are one of the most historically and universally observable market obstacles, but there is an ongoing—if recently challenged—assumption among economic historians that usury merely created a legal interest-rate ceiling with no effect on actual interest rates.[15] It is rare to find loan contracts that clearly discount the principal—a practice by which the amount of interest is deducted from the principal before it is lent. Not many contracts in the data from 1850 and 1860 show evidence of this, although there is one example of a mortgage loan for Mex$108 at 0 percent interest recorded on August 4, 1860. The loan was a four-month contract, and it is quite likely that it was a Mex$100 loan, for which a 2 percent per month interest rate was discounted up front.[16] Examples such as this one are so rare that it is much more likely that the usury restraints were respected in the official record and that they did constitute a real limit to interest rates and to the raising of capital through mortgages. New research in Britain and the United States also suggests that legal rates were effective and respected and that, as in nineteenth-century Yucatán, evading usury restraints was neither common nor easy.[17] Dodging these limits might not have been impossible, and it might have even been widespread in extra-official contracts and personal loans, but we have significant evidence that the legal market responded to positive incentives such as the growth of the henequen economy and the effect of the repeal of usury laws.[18]

The results in fig. 3.1 illustrate this reaction to the incentives in the mortgage market. Interest rates in 1850 and 1860 were controlled, and the few mortgage contracts in those years often did not state an interest rate at all, which further contributes to the sharp jump in 1870. Most contracts after the liberalization of interest rates had explicit rates that were well above the previous usury limits.

Once the laws criminalizing usury were abolished, interest rates increased well above the previous usury maximum. As soon as the usury ceilings were lifted in 1861 and reinforced in 1867, the market quickly reflected the change. Not only did interest rates rise quickly in the 1870s, but henequen production also started growing right around this time. The McCormick mechanical binder, designed specifically to use Yucatán henequen twine, was commercially released to great fanfare in the United

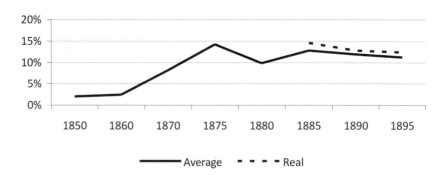

Fig. 3.1   Average and real interest rates, Mérida mortgages
SOURCE: Protocolos notariales, AGEY and ANEY.
NOTE: Real interest rates adjusted using Gómez-Galvarriato and Musacchio's "Un nuevo índice."

States in 1878.[19] The binder's success in the midwestern fields of the United States and Canada triggered the henequen boom, but it is difficult to imagine that the local credit market could have reacted the way it did but for the changes brought under the 1857 Constitution, the Reform Laws, and the 1861 decree. Without these legal changes, the price of credit would have remained at the maximum of 6 percent, which in a context of growing demand for credit, could not have represented the real cost of the risk to the lender.

The abolishment of usury restraints, coupled with the revision of the notarial code under the 1865 Ley Orgánica del Notariado y del Oficio de Escribano, also modernized the context in which mortgage contracts were recorded. These codes ushered the formal transformation of the contracts that mark Yucatán's transition to modern capital markets. Within ten years of this legal overhaul, almost all mortgage contracts contained two essential modern parameters of loans: an explicit interest rate and an explicit loan length. Fig. 3.2 charts the evolution of these parameters in the mortgage contracts.

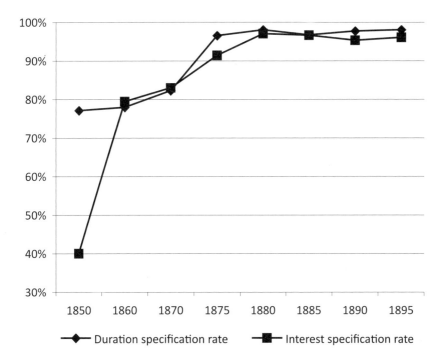

Fig. 3.2 Contracts with explicit duration and interest rates
SOURCE: Protocolos notariales, AGEY and ANEY.

This transition is significant because knowing both how much the loan would cost and when it would be repaid were essential pieces of information for both the lender and the borrower. The paucity of interest rate or duration specifications in the mortgage contracts in the 1850s and 1860s and the small amounts borrowed during this period (the total amounts borrowed in 1850 and 1860 were half of those borrowed in 1870) would indicate that the size of this market was determined by the legal limits on interest rates and the transactional costs of evading those limits.

It took at least a decade for the Reform Laws and their amendments related to church wealth and usury provisions to spread throughout the mortgage market and transcend the hiatus caused by Maximilian's reign. The instability in Mexico's political and legal climate is a likely reason for the slow reaction to the legal change. But once the situation stabilized and the mortgage market adjusted to the legal changes, the market was an almost perfectly inverted image of what it had been in 1850. All contracts stated interest rates, and most interest rates were well above the pre-1861 maximum of 6 percent. This suggests that institutional changes brought forth under the Reform Laws had significant effects on the mortgage market and on the credit market in general.

The Personal Credit Market

The gradual change in the recording of interest rates in mortgage contracts reflects not only the legal changes affecting interest rate and loan duration specifications but also the market response to the changes in economic conditions. The laws abolishing usury restrictions and imposing disclosure minimums on contracts date to the middle and late 1860s, and as fig. 3.1 illustrates, interest rates started growing from then on. Fig. 3.2 shows the increasing number of contracts with explicit duration times and interest rates, but it does not show how this change progressed among the mortgage contracts in each period for which we have data. The proportional shift in interest rates over the period is demonstrated in fig. 3.3, which charts the gradual transition of the credit market as it adapted to legal and economic shifts.

Fig. 3.3 breaks down the interest rates in the data set of mortgages into four categories. The first category represents contracts that had 0 percent or no stated interest rate. The second represents contracts that explicitly stated an interest rate greater than zero and up to, but not including, 6 percent (the legal interest rate according to civil and ecclesiastical law un-

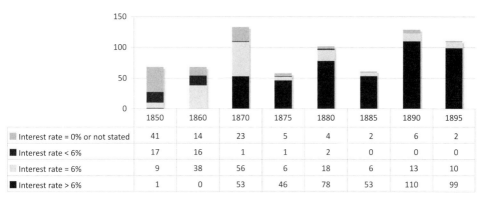

	1850	1860	1870	1875	1880	1885	1890	1895
Interest rate = 0% or not stated	41	14	23	5	4	2	6	2
Interest rate < 6%	17	16	1	1	2	0	0	0
Interest rate = 6%	9	38	56	6	18	6	13	10
Interest rate > 6%	1	0	53	46	78	53	110	99

Fig. 3.3 Number of contracts by interest-rate category
SOURCE: Protocolos notariales, AGEY and ANEY.

til 1861). The third category represents all contracts with an interest rate of exactly 6 percent (the legal limit until 1861). The fourth category represents the number of contracts with a stated rate above 6 percent (illegal until 1861). Each bar in the graph shows the number of contracts for each category and is based on a nominal interest rate, because the primary concern here is in seeing the explicit specification of terms change over time.

The first and second columns illustrate the enforcement of usury laws before 1861—only one mortgage contract had interest rates above 6 percent. In 1850, 60 percent of mortgage contracts in Mérida did not carry an interest rate at all (or did not state any interest rate). The remaining 40 percent, except for one case, carried interest rates that never exceeded the usury ceiling of 6 percent. The effects of the Reform Laws and growing antiecclesiastical sentiment in commercial and economic matters were reflected in the credit contracts in 1860, when 80 percent of contracts carried an explicitly stated interest rate (although none broke the 6 percent barrier). Average interest rates gradually increased above 6 percent per year after 1860 (as fig. 3.1 illustrates). After 1875 few contracts charged less than 6 percent per year, and contracts without a stated interest rate became a rarity, never accounting for more than 5 percent of the total. This result shows the influence that laws had on formal respect and observance of the practice. As the laws on usury were lifted and Yucatán's henequen production boomed, the interest rates gradually increased to reflect the true cost of credit in the nineteenth century.

The fall in the number of contracts without interest is also a reflection of the waning influence of the church in credit matters. In 1850 only 40 percent of contracts stated an interest rate, but by 1870 more than 80 percent of all contracts were explicit about their cost. Within these twenty years, not only did contracts become overwhelmingly explicit about interest rates, but the interest rate categories also shifted dramatically. In 1850 and 1860, only one contract charged more than 6 percent. By 1870 more contracts started to near that maximum, as 60 percent of contracts were at or below 6 percent (or the interest rate was not stated). Almost one-fifth of the contracts were still silent about their interest rate (17 percent of contracts charged no explicit interest rate).

By 1875 the figures start to reflect a radical shift, brought on by the restoration of the republic, the shift in legal requirements, the weakening of the church, and the start of economic growth: 79 percent of contracts charged an interest rate higher than 6 percent, and the few contracts that did not accounted for a very small proportion of amounts lent. The effect of the beginning of the boom is apparent, as not only were the explicit interest rates higher, but more money was being lent. Fig. 3.4 measures the proportion of loans in the same categories as fig. 3.3, relative to the value of each loan. It shows a similar trend to that of fig. 3.3; namely, as interest increased and became explicit, greater amounts of money were lent.

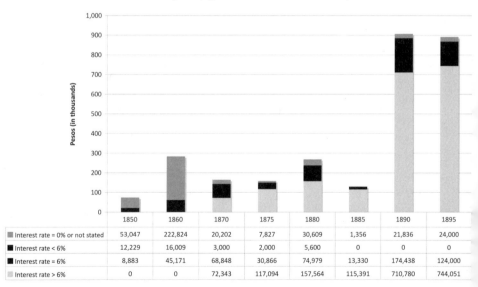

	1850	1860	1870	1875	1880	1885	1890	1895
Interest rate = 0% or not stated	53,047	222,824	20,202	7,827	30,609	1,356	21,836	24,000
Interest rate < 6%	12,229	16,009	3,000	2,000	5,600	0	0	0
Interest rate = 6%	8,883	45,171	68,848	30,866	74,979	13,330	174,438	124,000
Interest rate > 6%	0	0	72,343	117,094	157,564	115,391	710,780	744,051

Fig. 3.4 Proportion of sums lent by interest-rate category
SOURCE: Protocolos notariales, AGEY and ANEY.

In 1850, 60 percent of all mortgages did not charge interest. By 1875 more than 70 percent of mortgage loan amounts (in pesos) cost the borrowers more than 6 percent per year. In short, as demand for credit increased, so did the price of credit, especially because it could now legally rise to reflect the demand and risk. The fact that the rise in interest rates does not seem to have led to a fall in the demand for credit in Yucatán confirms the pent-up demand for credit, which had been created as much by the usury restraints as by the economic revival promoted by henequen.

Comparing the progression of interest rates in fig. 3.1 with the rise in contract disclosure reflected in fig. 3.2 illustrates the effect of the end of the church's influence on credit allocation. This change coincided with a sharp increase in the recording of interest rates, and this emphasis on clarity and transparency is perhaps one of the most modern features of the Yucatán market at this time.

The rising proportion of contracts with explicit interest rates illustrates the church's waning influence on civil contract law. In this light we can see the mute interest rates in the contracts of the 1850s, 1860s, and 1870s as a response to the usury bans. The cost of lending in earlier decades had been limited to 6 percent, or lenders found other ways of getting paid a rate high enough to warrant the risk of lending. As the laws changed to allow formally what might have been happening informally, implicit interest rates became explicit. Once the usury provisions were eliminated and the notarial function was firmly codified in specific laws, the services that notaries provided to their clients became formalized, public, and explicit.

With price controls lifted, lenders and borrowers in Yucatán experienced the freedom to indebt themselves in legal and explicit ways. Without banks or stock markets, the notaries became intermediaries, providing the contracts and contacts in a debt market created by the end of usury. This market would likely not have existed were it not for the structural changes in the economy, and the preeminence of mortgages as vehicles of finance can primarily be linked to the legal change that removed the price ceiling for credit.

The end of usury alone did not create the market, but it made this market function within modern parameters. The elimination of usury restraints removed one of the last formal vestiges of the colonial period from Mexico's economic system. Freely determined and unhampered interest rates and the development of credit markets were not the sole drivers of

Yucatán's nineteenth-century development, but it is difficult to imagine the financing of the Yucatán boom under price controls or under the transactional complications of implicit interest rates.

Other Debts and Markets

Mortgages recorded by notaries were not the only form of debt in Yucatán, or in Mexico. Banks, once they opened, extended long-term loans. Personal loans also were an important part of the world of debt in the nineteenth century. Family members lent to each other, employees borrowed from their employers, and employers owed their employees, especially on remote or cash-strapped haciendas. This world of debt existed alongside the mortgage market, in a realm of social relations that were no less binding than the ones encompassed in the mortgage contracts in the notarial ledgers. However, the records of these debts are more circumstantial. Bank loans are part of an institutional and often aggregate record, whereas personal loans survive in letters, wills, and if a debt is outstanding at the death of the lender or borrower, in probate accounts. Daily accounting of haciendas also yields information about the interconnectedness of personal and financial relationships that workers and employers developed in Yucatán and the permeability of debt across the social and ethnic spectrum.

Banks

A planter who decided in 1875 to grow henequen committed to a significant investment of time and money. Each henequen plant required between seven to eight years to mature for the first harvest, after which the plant could yield henequen *pencas* (as the leaves are called in Spanish) for fifteen to twenty years. Unless a planter was independently wealthy, the availability of long-term credit was crucial for the cultivation of a plant such as henequen that had a very long lead time. Absent banks and apart from mortgages, there were a variety of other long-term debt instruments available in the nineteenth century, especially to traders who financed part of their business with *cartas de crédito* (letters of credit), *pagarés* (IOUs), and other short-term credit instruments.[20] These debt instruments usually had short durations (between one month and one year) and guaranteed delivery of goods during the transportation delays between the port and final destination. These short-term notes were not recorded by notaries or kept in ledgers; they existed as long as the debt was unpaid and were destroyed with repayment.

Notaries did record ecclesiastical credit, but this was not a significant source of finance in Yucatán. During the colonial times the church funded many agricultural projects backed by real estate collateral, but the church in Yucatán was not as important a lender as colonial studies of church credit in other parts of Mexico have indicated.[21] On the other hand, mortgage loans between private citizens did become a sizable source of credit for Yucatecan planters and businesses.

Eventually though, economic growth in Yucatán would lead to the creation of formal financial institutions. The creation of banks was supported in part by the Commercial Code of 1884, which set out to institutionalize the country's commercial system. The code set out only vague national banking regulations, to which scholars point as the cause of Mexico's centralized and limited banking development during the nineteenth century.[22] The banking regulations did allow the charter of local banks, and more important, they allowed these banks to issue notes, solving a liquidity problem in the cash-strapped local economy.[23]

The Banco Nacional de México opened a small representative office in Mérida in 1882, and in late 1889, two local lending banks—the Banco Mercantil de Yucatán and the Banco Yucateco—opened to help finance the growing trade of henequen, add liquidity to a cash-poor economy, and raise equity for a developing infrastructure. The Banco Mercantil de Yucatán was the first financial institution in the state, opening its offices in late 1889, a few months ahead of the Banco Yucateco. Its main shareholders were the owners of the leading trading house at the time, Eusebio Escalante e Hijo. Financed by the rival trading house of Olegario Molina, the Banco Yucateco opened on February 1, 1890. The Banco Mercantil de Yucatán and the Banco Yucateco became the largest financial backers of the henequen fortune, but not before mortgages had become the most important source of long-term funds in the region. The first mortgage bank in Yucatán, the Banco Hipotecario de Yucatán y Campeche opened even later, in 1897. These mortgage banks were chartered under a separate statute than the banks and were not granted note-issuance privileges, and they were prohibited from charging more than 7 percent interest rate per year.

Mortgage banks were not a significant source of credit in the region, and if we compare the activity of these two commercial banks with the loans recorded in Mérida's notarial offices, it becomes even more apparent just how important notaries were in the provision of long-term credit in Yucatán.

Banks were created in Mexico largely as banks of issue and transfer, facilitating the short-term transactions of trading houses. Their role in this respect is clear in the graph, as they enter the Yucatán market in 1890 and immediately issue a significant number of short-term trade loans. This made them important additions to the Yucatecan financial stage, but in terms of long-term finance, mortgage loans in notarial offices were far bigger, more important, and more historically entrenched than those transacted through banks (see fig. 3.5).

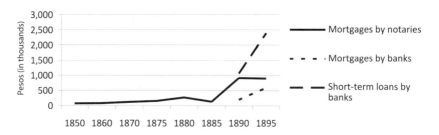

Fig. 3.5 Banks versus notaries
SOURCE: Protocolos notariales, AGEY and ANEY; "Balance promedio de bancos."

Labor Markets and Debts

Financing the henequen boom also required financing labor, an area that has received considerable attention. The shortage of labor in Yucatán prompted some plantation owners and overseers to engage in coercive and abusive labor arrangements, making this period, in the eyes of Yucatán's historians, one of the cruelest.[24] The interpretations differ, however, as to the extent of the abuse of land workers during this period, and the literature is split on this issue. On one side are those who compare debt peonage to slavery, who see the gradual encroachment of haciendas on village lands, indentured servitude, sharecropping, and paternalistic relations between plantation owners and laborers as a return to colonial traditions.[25] Others consider the labor changes as reflective of an environment in which labor was scarce, in which servants' debts represented assets to the plantation, and where paternalistic relationships did not necessarily translate into indenture or immobility. The servant's debt was a formal commitment to the hacienda, and if the servant remained on the hacienda while the debt was being repaid, the hacienda was assured the labor of one more worker.[26] This was not always the case, and it was not an enforceable commitment. Newspaper reports of peons who had left a hacienda with accrued debts are evidence of this exception.

The workers' debts incurred on henequen plantations were a crucial element of the henequen economy. Unlike mortgages, the debts incurred by workers at the hacienda shop (*tienda de raya*) or directly from the hacienda owner were never recorded by notaries. What evidence remains of these debts was recorded in private hacienda account books or records. As a documentary source, these records are found mostly within probate inventory proceedings and can often present the amount of unpaid debts owed hacienda owners at the time of their death, including debts owed by their employees. Like short-term trade credit, the notes stating the existence of a loan would most likely have been destroyed if the loan had been repaid. The probates list outstanding debts as unpaid assets or unrecoverable debts.

Debt peonage has been blamed for many of the abuses perpetrated against hacienda laborers, but the system inscribed itself in a complex relationship of reciprocal exchange and labor scarcity. Occasionally, the debts could even be owed *to* the workers, as in the case of Francisco Bolio's estate, discussed shortly. The extent to which debt permeated the relationships on the hacienda suggests that repayment was perhaps not as important as the relationship around which the loans developed.[27]

Ethnicity and Labor

Maya laborers owed the bulk of hacienda debts. These records provide a rare glimpse into the importance of debt in the life of rural workers, who were overwhelmingly Maya and who were otherwise completely absent from the history of the mortgage market in the henequen boom. In an illustrative historical turn, Maya debt survives most visibly in the probate inventories of wealthier hacienda owners who recorded their servants' debts. Unlike commercial mortgage debts, which were recorded under the heading of debt in the middle of the inventory ("*deudas activas y/o pasivas*"), servants' debts were accounted for in the real estate portion of the inventory. The accounting of these debts follows a logic that was common in labor-scarce economies and further supports an interpretation of these debts as labor-securing mechanisms. Under labor scarcity, servants' debts represented an asset to the hacienda, providing a guarantee that the servant would remain on the hacienda while in debt. This, of course, was not a foolproof method, because workers did leave, especially when they married and joined their spouse either on another hacienda or in a village or town.[28] Other workers staged outright escapes. Ads in the Mérida newspapers announced "missing workers" and called for the return of runaway peons.

In the probate inventories, servants' debts also provided a measure of the available workforce on a hacienda, which in turn was part of its productive potential. In estimating the worth of an estate, all components of an estate's assets and liabilities were counted, and workers' debts were part of the total. Francisco Bolio's probate reflects this accounting practice. He died a rich man in 1888 at the age of seventy-four. He was a member of the prosperous Bolio family, which owned numerous properties and became very involved in the henequen boom. Many of his family members appeared in the notarial ledgers as borrowers and lenders. In 1870 Francisco borrowed a relatively small amount of Mex$2,800 from Josefa Ruiz del Hoyo, to whom he paid 12 percent interest during the two-year duration of the contract. The loan was guaranteed by his three haciendas, and according to the record, he didn't pay the loan back until 1876, four years after it was due.[29]

He still owned these three haciendas when he died, and the probate inventory lists every piece of furniture inside the houses as well as the cattle and the fields of henequen, which were the basis of his wealth. Each separate hacienda had its own inventory, and each of these inventories included a list of workers' debts. The debts of workers who had left the hacienda without paying were listed on the liabilities side of the inventory, deemed to be unrecoverable. The breakdown of his workers' debts on each hacienda can be seen in table 3.1.

Table 3.1 Workers' debts in Francisco Cornelio Bolio's probate inventory (pesos)

Hacienda Xmatkuil	2,819.12
Hacienda Haltuncheb	1,300.50
Hacienda Canaca	481.87
Runaway Workers' Debts	337.74

SOURCE: Inventario Francisco Cornelio Bolio, Fondo Poder Civil, AGEY.

The total debt owed by his estate was about Mex$31,000, and the final account of assets yielded Mex$126,682; the servants' debts to the estate were a relative pittance. As mentioned earlier, Bolio's estate also owed some of his workers. These were most probably back-owed salaries in the amount of Mex$400 due five women with Maya surnames. The debts of Juana Tzun, Venancia Euan, Antonia Bacab, Florentina Cauich, and Anselma Cocom had originally been recorded in a *documento privado* (private document), probably a letter or a simple note.

It took a retinue of lawyers, clerks, and notaries more than nine months to create the probate documents of Bolio's estate and then start the redistribution among his heirs. Between March and November 1888, while the probate documents were being compiled, the daily accounting of his haciendas became part of the probate procedure. Sometimes a probate took a long time to resolve, especially when the estate was very large and included working haciendas with employees, factories (as the henequen-rasping buildings were called), and a large number of cattle that also worked on the fields. In these cases, not only was the value more difficult to estimate, but the estate also needed to be maintained while the probate proceedings were taking place. To safeguard the value of the estate prior to its dissolution, a trustee was named to run the haciendas in the interim. This trustee kept an exact account of all outflows and inflows of the haciendas, and these accounts became part of the probate inventory.[30] These accounts in the *cuenta de administración* of Francisco Bolio's probate inventory provide a perspective into the income and indebtedness of hacienda workers, who were mostly Maya and for whom not much had changed since the colonial period.

Mayas participated in Yucatán's economy as more than just cheap labor, especially if they lived in Mérida or one of its nearby towns. Mayas there were often small landowners, and even if they were absent from the mortgage market, the nineteenth-century Maya community was not entirely absent from the world of credit. José María Cuxim illustrates this point. He was a relatively wealthy man of Maya descent with an estate that inventories at nearly Mex$5,000, larger than many of the estates probated in Mérida and elsewhere among non-Mayas.[31] Cuxim had died in 1888, leaving his wife Teresa López as a widow. Their four children were all adults, and the probate was initiated at the behest of his eldest son, who was the administrator of the estate for the length of its dissolution. His probate opens with a detailed list of the expenses incurred by his lawyer, Juan Molina Solís.

The estate included mostly gold trinkets and jewelry and Cuxim's ancestral home in Izamal, which was worth Mex$3,151. This house had not been part of the joint marital property, as described in the probate. The Mex$1,600 of joint assets was duly divided in two: 50 percent to Cuxim's widow and the other 50 percent divided among his children. The home in Izamal was sold, and the remaining furniture and decorative pieces became part of the estate. The income resulting from the sale of the house and the precise accounting of the value of each item was then distributed equally among the five heirs.[32] José María Cuxim did not die owing money to anyone, nor did anyone owe him money.

Cuxim was hardly representative of the Maya population, although he may represent the Maya elites who prevailed throughout the colonial and independent period. Marcos Chalé, on the other hand, was an urban laborer in Mérida, employed in trades and crafts, as were many urban Mayas. He had taken out a Mex$2,000 loan with interest (the interest rate was not mentioned in the proceedings) from Manuel Pinelo Montero.[33] Demetrio Molina guaranteed the loan and also initiated the court proceedings after Chalé's death to compel Nestora Escamilla, Chalé's wife, to pay back the loan. The case documents state that Chalé admitted his outstanding debt to Pinelo Montero on his deathbed, but no documentary evidence is provided to substantiate the existence of this loan. The courts ruled against the plaintiff and protected Chalé's widow, aborting any attempt by the plaintiff to value Chalé's estate with a probate.

Poverty among Mayas and everyone else in the sample of probates analyzed did not preclude debt. Even the smaller Maya probates include outstanding loans, although few of these loans were secured by a mortgage contract or any sizable collateral and were instead informally remembered and recorded in the probate by the surviving parties.

Among these smaller probates, for example, Felipe Moo's probate shows that he had died with Mex$293 in listed assets and Mex$67 in liabilities. His probate inventory is strikingly simple, limited to a summary account of the value of his real estate and his cattle. As for the liabilities, the inventory lists how much was owed and to whom: Mex$7 owed in labor to Sóstenes Silveira; Mex$50 to José Inés Pérez, which were to be repaid in kind with bales of henequen; and Mex$10 owed to José Isabel Cauich. Also Maya, Cauich had left these Mex$10 on reserve with Moo, to be saved for the day Cauich got married.[34]

Moo's debts suggest three realities for Mayas in the Yucatán market. First, the dearth of cash and labor in Yucatán is reflected in the debt for labor to Sóstenes Silveira. This reality was common to the rest of the market, as the workers' debts in the hacienda records of Francisco Bolio illustrate. Second, the payment in kind owed to José Inés Pérez proposes a perspective on the involvement of Mayas in the henequen economy that went beyond providing hard labor for the henequen haciendas. Mayas such as Moo were also independent farmers and laborers, making the best use of the small plot of land they owned. Like many people who lived in Yucatán and were not wealthy henequen plantation owners, Mayas and mestizos put their backyards and vacant lots to their most efficient use by including a few rows of corn for tortillas and a few plants of henequen for cash. Third and most relevant, Cauich's Mex$10 deposit with Moo hints at a parallel world of credit and saving. Moo held Cauich's savings, and Cauich could call it back at an undetermined time. Perhaps Moo kept the money, literally saving it for Cauich's wedding day, or Moo put that money to productive use in the meantime. Either way, this piece of evidence and the long list of gold *escudos y aretes* (medals and earrings) listed under the assets in José María Cuxim's probate suggest that Mayas held wealth, saved it, and invested it. In the case of Cuxim's gold jewelry, he secured his wealth in fungible assets, making it easier to distribute later among his heirs; the Mex$10 deposit in Moo's inventory reveals the existence of an alternative lending mechanism among Mayas that unfolded separately from the loans recorded by notaries.

It remains that Moo and Cauich and most of the 128 Maya probates sampled represent the poorer members of society, reinforcing the notion that the inequality of wealth in Yucatán affected Mayas much more, and more obviously, than Yucatecans with Spanish last names.[35] It also reinforces the fact that inequality left many out of the credit market, and the experience in this economy for people with Maya surnames is an illustrative example of the experience of all poor and marginalized people, whatever their ethnicity.

Chapter Four

What Do Notaries Do?
The Formal and Informal Roles of Notaries

A man enjoys a good name and reputation among his peers when he accomplishes
his duties justly and strictly; without a good name the authority that the law
conveys to a notary would lack its most precious and solid base.
—*El novísimo escribano instruido*, 1859

A golden name is better than a golden bed.
—Mexican proverb

The agricultural boom altered Yucatán's financial infrastructure, and notaries became the conduits to long-term finance in the state. While large
agricultural trading houses secured trade credit from foreign brokers, and
smaller producers raised short-term credit with letters of credit and IOUs,
long-term credit continued to be a personal transaction. Mortgages were
the most reliable and enforceable personal credit loans because they were
secured by collateral and recorded by a notary. Although the mortgage
contract was only one of the many forms of debt credit instruments available in Yucatán, it was one of the few to survive in the historical archive.
Personal debts, unlike mortgages, were not recorded systematically. Although they occasionally appear in probate records or wills, personal debts
were recorded as evidence of unpaid debts. Commercial credit also suf-
fered from a lack of systematic recording. An IOU, for example, may have
been written on a sheet of paper and kept safe until it was repaid. As a
general rule an IOU was neither registered nor kept with a third party, and
therefore, it is rare to find this sort of document in the historical archive.
Mortgage contracts, on the other hand, were recorded by a third party—a
notary, who kept the original version of each contract in bound ledgers,
whereby the evidence of the debt existed not only until the debt was repaid

but long afterward in the ledger that became an enduring historical record. These records allow a historian to trace almost all mortgages ever recorded by notaries in Yucatán, and not only the ones that remained outstanding. This chapter unfolds the role of notaries in this market, from the legal rules determining their civil role to the act of recording the mortgages in their offices and the interactions that happened in between. The first part assesses the notary's formal role, as defined in legal and notarial codes. The second part develops the informal role of notaries and its significance in the development of the mortgage market.

The Formal Role of Notaries

The civil procedure of Mexico was based on Roman law, imported by the colonial Spanish rule, and gave notaries an integral role in the legal system, which had relied on written documentation since the colonial period. Also called *escribanos* (scribes) during this period, notaries recorded the procedures, documents, and contracts of colonial society. They traveled to the Americas in the sixteenth century with Hernán Cortés, who dictated his first reports on his arrival to Mexico to his scribe, Diego de Godoy.[1] Throughout the colonial period, scribes stood at the center of civil, penal, and ecclesiastical record keeping. Scribes were classified according to three different functions related to the offices for which they were keeping records: (1) *escribanos reales* (royal scribes) were attached to royal courts or offices in the colonies; (2) public notaries such as the *escribanos mayores de armada* (army scribes) or the *escribanos de entradas de las cárceles* (scribes who recorded the arrival of conscripts to the prisons) were attached to public institutions; and (3) the *escribanos de número* were assigned numbered offices and recorded the contracts for the civilian population. All notaries were trained in the same way, but once assigned, the differences among them were dictated by the kind of documents they recorded and the social and institutional context in which they worked. Their title was conferred by the Spanish Crown, and the numbered notarial offices were the only ones that were salable and transferable.

In the postcolonial and modern period, the office of the notary was divided into two main categories: national notaries (equivalent to the royal scribes) and public notaries (who owned their numbered offices).[2] The granting of the title was transferred in 1863 to the judicial power of the French occupation, which would prove to have indelible effects on the formal role of scribes, who by then were referred to as *notarios*. The Mexican Congress enacted the first comprehensive postcolonial notarial code under Maximilian—a code that has served as the model for each successive notarial code ever since. The Ley Orgánica del Notariado y del Oficio de Escribano established clear rules for notarial function and made them applicable throughout the entire nation. The law formalized the use of the term "notary," which could refer only to the head of the notarial office, while "scribe" referred to a notary's assistant, who was allowed to sign documents that did not involve high value or large amounts of property but could not act independently of the notary. Increasing the record-keeping responsibility of notaries, the law also mandated that the notarial office keep a copy of all contracts signed by the notary or assistants together with an inventory or an index of the documents. The 1865 code further standardized the notary's duties across the country by requiring each office to display a map of the Mexican Empire, a map of the city in which the office was situated, and a list of all notaries, scribes, agents, and judges whose documents were in the office's records. The new code established the necessary components of legal public documents recorded by notaries, requiring the name, birthplace, residence, civil status, and occupation of each party to a contract; a detailed explanation of the contract; and the signatures of all parties and witnesses, as well as that of the notary.

The 1865 law formalized the duty of the colonial scribe and brought the formal function of Mexican notaries closer to that of their French counterparts. The law reinforced the educational requirements of notaries, who even before the 1865 code received education similar to that of lawyers. The notary-to-be was required to study civil law, be trained in the writing and keeping of public documents, and undergo an apprenticeship with a notary, judge, or lawyer. The 1865 law further tied the notaries' training to that of lawyers; Maximilian's notarial code stipulated that notaries had to take preparatory courses for a career in the judicial system and then a two-year course on notarial law, as well as perform a two-year apprenticeship at another notary's office. Moreover, they were required to take and pass a handwriting class, which perhaps explains the surprising similarity in handwriting among notaries. Aspiring notaries in Mexico City had to present their qualifications and application to the Colegio de Escribanos (notarial college). Apprentices in other states and territories, including Yucatán, could become notaries simply by presenting their completed exams and degrees to the local ministry of justice and superior tribunal courts.[3] This last step conferred the title of notario. The assignment to a particular notarial office was determined by the local civil court (in Yucatán this would have been in Mérida), which allocated the offices as they became available.[4]

In contrast to the European notarial tradition that allowed offices to be handed down through generations, each notarial office in Mexico was assigned to one specific notary, who had the right to sell or transfer the office to another notary, something that usually occurred at the end of a notary's career. Yucatán did not have a notarial school (the main one, the Colegio de Escribanos, was in Mexico City), but its notaries-in-training studied at the local law school, the Escuela de Jurisprudencia de Yucatán, which conferred the credentials that the notarial school in Mexico City required of all notaries.

Notaries charged fees for their services to maintain their office and pay their employees; notaries often hired assistants (some of whom were apprenticing notaries) and clerks, who often appeared as witnesses on notarial contracts. State congressional budgets established fee schedules for notarial documents, because recording such documents were considered public services. The contracts recorded by a notary never indicated whether the fees were in accordance with those outlined in the congressional papers, as records of fees were kept in a separate ledger of accounts, which were not part of the public record and have not appeared among the surviving archival documents. References to notarial fees are also scant, except in the case of civil court documents, which occasionally mention the administrative costs of a case. Notarial expenses were clearly outlined, suggesting that the fees were fixed and not based on commission.[5] The amount paid for a notary's signature as witness to a document, for example, would include the Mex$1.87 tax paid on the document, the notary's fee of Mex$2.00 to witness said document, Mex$2.13 for notarial stamps, and Mex$1.63 for the registration cost of the document.[6]

Notaries were respectable members of the legal profession—learned and literate men whose participation in legal affairs was usually limited to the recording and witnessing of documents and contracts. Most of them lived and worked in Mérida, where they dealt with clients from a very broad social spectrum. Impoverished day laborers recorded the sale of their small plot of land at the notary's office; widows countersigned the guardianship of their children's inheritance to their deceased husband's brothers; and landowners registered labor contracts with new hires.

Notaries recorded everything, including land sales, labor contracts, guardianships, business associations, wills and testaments, and credit contracts.

Moreover, notaries' records of these contracts with their signature on them made the contracts legal and enforceable; the notary's signature on the documents and its record in the notary's ledgers represented the agreement between the parties and the legality of that agreement. Obtaining this signature was not a voluntary decision by the contract parties; they were required by law to use a notary to guarantee the legality of all contracts, especially concerning any real estate transactions. In that vein, any contracts that affected the integrity of the ownership of real estate or any type of property had to be notarized, including wills, purchase agreements, and, of course, mortgages.[7]

The stricter definition of the duties of notaries codified under Maximilian in 1865 reinforced the administrative organization of notarial activity and maintained the notary's primacy in the property-recording process. As a consequence, while mortgages had to be recorded because they could affect the ownership of a parcel of land, loans that were not collateralized by land could not affect the ownership of land and therefore did not have to be recorded.[8] This division created an automatic separation among credit contracts: loans that were not collateralized with a plot of land or any other form of real estate were not legally required to be recorded in a notary's office. By the same token, uncollateralized loans, if unrecorded, did not benefit from the enforceability provided by the notarial contract.[9] As representatives of the *fe pública* (public faith), notaries conferred legitimacy to contracts because a notary's signature guaranteed judicial legitimacy, and the collateral built into these mortgages represented a legal promise not only to repay but also to transfer ownership of the collateralized land in case of default. The legal enforceability of contracts drawn up by notaries and the collateral in the case of mortgages reduced the risk of nonrepayment and facilitated the enforcement of contracts. This enforceability, coupled with the legal proviso for the recording of mortgages, was at the heart of the notarial role in mortgage markets.

The focus on collateral had its roots in the liberal Reform Laws, which, beginning in 1859, had intended to modernize landownership and reduce the landed wealth of the church. Wishing to leave behind the backwardness associated with their colonial past, liberal governments had enforced the gradual confiscation and sale of ecclesiastical, communal, and village lands.[10] Not only did Maximilian not interrupt that process, but he also supported throughout Mexico the creation of large haciendas made up of the previously broken-up parcels of cattle ranches, village lands, and any piece of land that was or seemed uncultivated. Benito Juárez enacted the

1870 Civil Code, which only reinforced the effects of the Reform Laws and Maximilian's equally liberal intentions. The effect in Yucatán in the wake of the henequen boom was to inflate the price of and demand for land and increase the need for credit.

The 1870 Civil Code incorporated many of the changes initiated under Maximilian. Although Maximilian and Juárez stood on opposite sides of a political minefield, both shared similar views in terms of legal and economic policies in the spirit of the laws that should structure the civil and commercial interactions of a modern nation. The code also required mortgages to be recorded publicly, which gradually led to the creation of regional public records offices. The code also established that mortgages needed to be specific, meaning that specific assets needed to be specified as collateral, rather than as a customary general reference to assets owned by the debtor. The specification requirement—including the length of the contract, the statute of limitation in case of default or late payment, and the irreversibility of the legal decision in case of default and litigation—all contributed to strengthening the legal enforceability of mortgages as a credit instrument.

The relationship between notaries and clients built up over years. People needed a notary's service at many times in their lives—when they inherited a piece of land, sold their home, made a loan, entered into a business association with a partner, or signed their will. The important personal and business relationships that notaries had with their lenders and borrowers marked the mortgage market and developed over time. Not surprisingly, three of the most active notaries in Mérida's mortgage market also had very long careers. Table 4.1 charts the careers of these notaries and their colleagues and competitors between 1850 and 1895. All notaries (except the ones who barely recorded mortgages) are represented here. Column 1 accounts for the number of years each of these notaries was actively recording mortgages and other contracts. Columns 2 and 3 mark the span of their careers. The names of the three leading notaries in the mortgage market—Manuel Ávila Maldonado, Carlos Aranda, and José Anacleto Patrón Zavalegui—appear in boldface.

Table 4.2 complements table 4.1 and accounts for each notary's share of the total mortgage activity.[11] The first row in the table accounts for the total peso amount of mortgages transacted in a particular year. The table highlights three characteristics of the notarial market in Mérida. First, notaries did not always have mortgages to record: notaries who did not appear from sampled year to sampled year did not disappear from Mérida;

Table 4.1   Active years of recording mortgages per notary between 1850 and 1895

	Number of years active	Span of years mortgages were recorded	
		First contract	Last contract
Manuel Ávila Maldonado	39	1856	1895
Manuel Barbosa	30	1850	1880
Gregorio Pérez Escarrega	30	1862	1892
Carlos Aranda	28	1861	1889
José Anacleto Patrón Zavalegui	24	1875	1899
José Anacleto Patrón	23	1855	1878
José María Sánchez	22	1871	1893
Francisco Flota	20	1864	1884
Gumersindo Poveda	19	1850	1869
José Calbeto	18	1850	1868
Joaquín María Mendoza	16	1850	1866
Francisco Rojas	16	1860	1876
José Ceferino Aguilar	15	1861	1876
José María Río	12	1858	1870
Eligio Guzmán	12	1872	1884
José Andrade	12	1884	1896
José Dolores Aranda	12	1884	1896
Ladislao Cantón	11	1858	1869
Francisco del Río	10	1850	1860
José Dolores Rocha	9	1850	1859
Víctor Rendón	9	1868	1877
José Antonio Alayón	8	1869	1877
Eugenio del Rosario Patrón	5	1850	1855
Antonio Patrón	4	1850	1854
Miguel Acevedo	4	1890	1894
Manuel de la Calleja	3	1850	1853
Manuel Fernández	3	1850	1853

SOURCE: Protocolos notariales, AGEY and ANEY.

NOTE: The year 1850 was probably not the first year of activity for Manuel Barbosa, José Calbeto, Manuel de la Calleja, Francisco del Río, Manuel Fernández, Joaquín María Mendoza, Antonio Patrón, Eugenio del Rosario Patrón, Gumersindo Poveda, and José Dolores Rocha, but it is the first year in which I started following them.

they just did not record any mortgages in those particular years. Among these notaries, mortgages were not a very large part of their business, and they did not have large stakes in the market itself, as the examples of José Anacleto Castillo and José María Sánchez suggest. In the four observed years of Castillo's activity, he never recorded more than about 13 percent of the market share of mortgages. Sánchez's share of the mortgage market increased from 2 percent in 1875 to 10 percent in 1890, but mortgages never became his specialty. Similar to most notaries, Castillo and Sánchez

Table 4.2 Notaries recording mortgages between 1850 and 1895

Notaries	Percentage of total share							
	1850	1860	1870	1875	1880	1885	1890	1895
Manuel Barbosa	1.74	27.18	7.44	5.67	—	—	—	—
Pedro José Canto	2.53	—	—	—	—	—	—	—
Manuel de la Calleja	1.64	—	—	—	—	—	—	—
Francisco del Río	3.06	9.06	—	—	—	—	—	—
Manuel Fernández	5.02	—	—	—	—	—	—	—
Pedro Irabien	0.67	—	—	—	—	—	—	—
Joaquín Mendoza	0.95	4.99	—	—	—	—	—	—
Antonio Patrón	22.91	—	—	—	—	—	—	—
Eugenio del Rosario Patrón	29.39	—	—	—	—	—	—	—
Gumersindo Poveda	1.34	—	—	—	—	—	—	—
José Dolores Rocha	19.96	—	—	—	—	—	—	—
Ladislao Cantón	—	17.54	—	—	—	—	—	—
José Anacleto Castillo	—	13.12	0.26	—	—	1.12	0.22	—
Manuel Ávila Maldonado	—	20.54	9.04	41.00	8.92	1.81	13.93	10.67
José María Río	—	7.57	3.61	—	—	—	—	—
Francisco Flota	—	—	37.79	—	47.66	—	0.57	—
Francisco Rojas	—	—	29.35	2.55	0.19	—	—	—

(continues)

Table 4.2 *(continued)*

Notaries	Percentage of total share							
	1850	1860	1870	1875	1880	1885	1890	1895
Tomás Ruiz	—	—	1.04	—	—	—	—	—
José Ceferino Aguilar	—	—	5.49	—	—	—	—	—
José Antonio Alayón	—	—	5.47	—	—	—	0.35	—
Carlos Aranda	—	—		10.19	25.56	16.39		—
Eligio Guzmán	—	—		30.97		0.23		—
José Anacleto Patrón Zavalegui	—	—		3.74	11.36	73.12	71.29	74.23
José María Sánchez	—	—		2.16	1.45	1.65	10.51	—
Tomás Aranda Arceo	—	—			3.40			—
José Dolores Torres Aranda	—	—			1.45	0.10		—
José Andrade	—	—				4.68	0.07	4.56
Gregorio Pérez Escarrega	—	—				0.32	2.29	0.91
Miguel Acevedo	—	—					0.02	—
Avelino López	—	—						0.18
Alfonso Peniche	—	—						9.41
Illegible	10.79	0	0.51	0.72	0.01	0.58	0.32	0.04
Total pesos lent	74,482	84,002	192,865	157,786	268,752	751,426	975,270	985,191

SOURCE: Protocolos notariales, AGEY and ANEY.

NOTE: The total volume of funds lent in a year represents the sum of all contracts recorded each year. For some years, a notary's ledger may be missing. In most cases, his share of the market (based on his share in the previous and successive years) is small and should not affect the market share distribution.

made their living from recording other transactions, such as land sales, wills and testaments, and all other manner of civil contracts. Second, while longevity mattered in developing relationships with clients, it was not necessarily correlated to market share in the mortgage market. To highlight this, five of the names of the notaries with the longest careers (from table 4.1) are in boldface. Third, the mortgage market tended toward concentration. As the Yucatán economy improved and Mérida's mortgage market grew with it, fewer notaries were handling an increasing number of transactions. As the century advanced, many notaries who had long been recording mortgages were being sidelined, and mortgage activity became more centralized in the offices of a handful of notaries.

Table 4.2 shows the breakdown of each notary's mortgage records (relative to all the mortgages recorded) in each sampled year. The breakdown shows each notary's percentage share of the mortgage-recording activity and also illustrates the fact that notaries did not transfer their offices to family members. Only one surname (Patrón) appears in the table throughout the years with different first names (three of them), and it isn't clear that Eugenio del Rosario Patrón or Antonio Patrón (who were recording mortgages in 1850) transferred their offices to work with Patrón Zavalegui, who became one of Mérida's main notaries. (Patrón Zavalegui also did not inherit their offices.) Some notaries recorded mortgages in one period and never reappeared in that capacity; for example, Manuel Fernández recorded a few mortgages in his 1850 ledger, and José Ceferino Aguilar recorded mortgages for his clients only in 1870. Other notaries were active for long periods of time, although none of the notaries active in 1850 appear in the records by 1890. Two notaries who were active in 1860, José Anacleto Castillo and Ávila Maldonado, were still recording mortgages in 1890, and in any given year more than half the notaries had been recording mortgages for ten years or more, with an average longevity (in terms of mortgage recording) for each notary of about seventeen years.[12]

Table 4.3 shows that near the end of the nineteenth century the market share of mortgage contracts was increasingly concentrated in the hands of a smaller number of notaries. Eleven notaries in Mérida recorded mortgages in 1850, and throughout the rest of the period the number of notaries active in a year ranged from six to nine.[13] This variation is largely due to the fact that not all notaries had clients who needed to borrow or lend through mortgage credit. While notaries recorded a wide variety of civil contracts, and a large proportion of the population would at some point or other require a notary's service, only a smaller proportion of the popula-

Table 4.3   Summary of active notaries handling mortgages in Mérida

	Number of notaries	Number of mortgage contracts	Top two notaries' share of the mortgage market (%) (in terms of pesos)
1850	11	70	52.30
1860	7	68	47.72
1870	9	135	67.14
1875	7	58	71.97
1880	8	103	73.22
1885	9	184	89.51
1890	9	129	85.22
1895	6	111	84.90

SOURCE: Protocolos notariales, AGEY and ANEY.

tion primarily drew on the mortgage market. Furthermore, except for 1860, only two notaries at a time consistently accounted for more than half of all credit contracts signed in Mérida. Column 1 aggregates the number of notaries recording mortgages, column 2 accounts for the number of mortgage contracts in any given year, and column 3 calculates the proportion of the total amounts lent through the mortgages that were recorded by the two notaries with the largest share of the mortgage market.[14]

Column 3 in table 4.3 suggests that notarial activity, as measured by the value of mortgages, had always been highly concentrated (nearing 50 percent in 1850 and 1860). This trend clearly increased as the economy's growth rate accelerated. By the century's end a growing number of the mortgages in Mérida were being recorded by two increasingly busy notaries, suggesting that a few notaries were interacting with an increasingly large group of people. In this context, the relationship of notaries with their clients, especially with respect to credit transactions, became more important. The reputation of each of these clients among other lenders and borrowers, as well as with the notary himself, became a linchpin mechanism of this market.

The Informal Role of Notaries

Notaries recorded contracts and supplied the legal backbone to social interaction ever since colonial times, but as Mérida's economy grew and ecclesiastical institutions dwindled, notaries also strengthened the relationship between their borrowers and lenders in a strategic way. Notaries became the link between lenders and borrowers not only because they were acquainted with them but also because notaries recorded the contracts, safeguarded them, and could present the contracts as proof of a client's record. Notaries became the first and last monitor of other people's property (because the notary was the one who recorded the sale transaction) and the informal recipient of information on property value, personal wealth, family businesses, and preferences. One of the notary's main contributions to the credit market was embodied in his most traditional function, namely as the scrivener and record keeper. This formal function was, however, complemented by the information the notary gained about his clients in the process of drawing up their contracts. The notary's main assets were his ledgers, where each transaction was formally recorded and stored, but a notary's wealth included the sense he gained informally about his clients. Unlike investment banks today, notaries were not subject to regulations that prevented them from using their knowledge about one client to benefit another. Even if parties to contracts had prior knowledge about each other, the notary probably knew more about one or both than either did about the other.

The law determined that de facto only a handful of people in any one town would become notaries, and in this way allowed only a few people to have a lot of information about everyone else in the community. The amount of information a notary had about his clients and his ability to use this information judiciously was both the currency of his worth in a community and the asset around which he competed against other notaries. The barriers to entering the profession created a closed pool of available notaries, and among these, the drive toward the centralization and concentration of power increased during the henequen boom, especially vis-à-vis mortgage contracts.

In countries with more developed formal financial systems, banks play the role of information brokers in credit transactions. Without banks, kinship networks can play the role of monitors and informal enforcers of moral codes, as we can still observe among current-day rotation credit associations as well as in nomadic communities.[15] In nineteenth-century Yucatán, notaries assumed both these roles as information brokers and monitors who created incentives for good behavior. Not only did notaries in Yucatán hold information about debts, collateral, and ownership in their ledgers, they also had significant amounts of information on their clients through other mundane interactions—guardianships, incorporations, contracts, land deeds, and wills. Notaries were constantly called on to record civil contracts and interactions, and as a consequence, they became the keepers of information about the current and historical value of collateral presented for a mortgage. They also held the documents guaranteeing the rightful ownership of the collateral and had additional information about any other liens on the collateralized property and assets of the borrower.

This information chain was tremendously valuable to lenders who relied on it for information about future borrowers, but the existence of this information chain also created incentives for borrowers to honor the terms of their contract, lest they be forever tainted in the notary's network. The personal relationship notaries developed with their clients while discovering these details gradually put notaries in an intermediary position to vouch informally for the reputation of anyone who had transacted regularly through their offices. The notary's role in this intermediation remained largely covert, because there were no official stipulations in the notarial codes about brokering of credit contracts or about advising in matters of financial affairs.

The evidence that notaries were acting on behalf of their clients or that they were providing financial advice is indisputable, if indirect.[16] The weakness of kinship ties, the strength of loyalty to notaries, and the depth of notaries' information about their clients all contributed to the development of their intermediary roles. Notaries did not act as brokers, investment bankers, or deposit banks, all of which were nonexistent in Yucatán and which, in other parts of the world, placed funds and deposits on behalf of investors.[17] Instead, notaries were intermediaries in this economy by providing competitive and efficient access to borrowers who could facilitate long-term credit that was not directly tied to the henequen trade. The law created immutable barriers to entry to the profession, and Mérida had at most and at any given time in the nineteenth century, fifteen notaries operating in the city. They were a small group among the Yucatecan society; the 1896 directory of Mérida lists more than sixty lawyers but only ten notaries. This small group, however, did not avail itself equally of the growth in lending. Some notaries were significantly more important in these transactions than others, and the important notaries became central figures in the Mérida mortgage market, while others barely registered a mortgage contract in the entire nineteenth century. Even though a small number of notaries became big in this market, kinship networks played almost no role.

Kinship does not explain the pattern of credit flows in Mérida during the late nineteenth century, although it was an important social glue in preindustrial Mérida. Family businesses and alliances were common, and the city's small population supports assumptions that the wealthiest lenders in Mérida would have been members of well-established trading or landowning families and that their alliances were bolstered by loans between family members.[18] While this may well have happened, there is no evidence of large intrafamily lending in the ledgers of notaries. This does not mean family members were not lending to one another, but that during the boom years they were not doing it through the mortgage contracts recorded by notaries.[19]

Kinship rates were relatively and marginally higher before the boom in 1850 and 1860, but the total amounts lent and borrowed were small, as were the number of borrowers and contracts. In this context, the kinship rates cannot be interpreted as a symbol of a strong kin-based lending tradition. If there was kinship-based lending in the later part of the century and during the henequen boom, they do not appear in the mortgage contracts in notarial records. And these loans, should they have existed, never made it into the probate record either. The absence of reliable evidence pointing to kinship makes it much more likely that kinship was not a determining variable in the mortgage market and that the connection between kinship and the mortgage market was tenuous. The number of contracts between kin was too low and waning, as table 4.4. illustrates.[20]

Table 4.4 Kinship bonds in mortgage credit contracts

	Mortgages between kin	Total mortgages	Proportion of mortgages between kin (%)
1850	8	70	11.43
1860	10	68	14.71
1870	6	135	4.44
1875	2	58	3.45
1880	3	103	2.91
1885	10	184	5.43
1890	9	129	6.98
1895	8	111	7.21

Source: Protocolos notariales, AGEY and ANEY.

Note: Kinship was established in two ways: (1) by seeing if the contract clearly states the family tie between parties or (2) by matching paternal and maternal last names for siblings and first cousins as well as in-laws.

In the notary's ledgers, most contracts were neither exclusively among the elite nor between family members. We know this because the contracts have so many direct and tacit references to family origin and because of the felicitous Mexican tradition of naming and recording both paternal and maternal last names, allowing an easy discovery of first-degree kin, siblings, parents and children, cousins, aunts and uncles, and nuclear in-laws, such as parents-in-law and siblings-in-law.[21]

The arrival of new lenders in the market in response to the dissolution of ecclesiastical power in the middle of the century provoked a shift in ownership, which was reflected in the notaries' ledger entries. As ecclesiastical loans were transferred to civilian lenders, and ecclesiastical property was sold off, the structure of Yucatán's economy changed. The wider economic changes caused by the rise in the price and production of henequen also contributed to the rise in the number of individual (and nonecclesiastical) lenders throughout the rest of the century, further diluting the need for kin contacts in loans. As the formal requirements of disclosure in contracts increased and as the credit market grew, kinship gradually became even less of a glue that bound lenders and borrowers. The importance of family ties in the framework of financial relations diminished, and in the changing economic and legal contexts, these transactions became more formal, allowing notaries to replace the bond of trust that kinship ties originally conveyed.

Kinship networks were not crucial to mobilize the financial resources we observe in the mortgage contracts. There may have been financial transfers between family members, but there is no way for us to trace them, because they happened outside of the notary's office. Occasionally these loans appear in probate records, but they cannot provide a reliable picture of the extent of nonmortgage intrafamily lending. Of course, some intrafamily lending was recorded, and one can only assume that when mortgages were written between family members, it was because the formal guarantee and the legal enforceability of the notarized contract mattered. The ties that bound family members occasionally needed to be reinforced institutionally—first, to secure repayment and, second, to guarantee some degree of family harmony.

One example of intrafamily credit lending that suggests kinship was not the key mechanism through which credit was allocated is the case of Joaquín Duarte Troncoso, who borrowed a substantial amount from his mother. This case highlights how the formalization of the loan, not the kinship tie, was the element that held the transaction together. Joaquin Duarte Troncoso had gone increasingly into debt as a henequen planter, and in early 1890 he borrowed thirty thousand pesos from his seventy-five-year-old mother, Concepción Troncoso. Joaquin had already borrowed from other people, as demonstrated by the note attached to the deed of the hacienda he offered as collateral. The lien check performed by the notary or one of his clerks confirmed these prior debts. As the notarial contract highlights, Concepción helped her son, but she also protected her estate; she did not give her son the privilege of an interest-free loan. Moreover, the loan to Joaquin carried an 8 percent interest rate and had a five-year maturity. Joaquin offered the hacienda with the existing lien as collateral, as well as another hacienda he owned in Mérida. Concepción also thought to protect the integrity of her estate and her other children by stipulating in the contract that if she were to die within the next five years (or before the loan was paid back), Joaquin's loan was to be repaid to Concepción's estate. In this case, while kinship might have eased Joaquin's access to his mother's capital, it did not relieve him of the obligations any borrower would have toward a lender.[22]

Although kinship bonds mostly disappeared between lenders and borrowers in the mortgage market, it did not imply that family did not matter in times of financial need. It does suggest, however, that while family members may have seemed like an obvious source of funds for cash-strapped borrowers, the emotional and economic costs of doing business with family might have made such options less attractive, especially if avenues of funding opened up that did not mix business with family. Joaquin Duarte Troncoso's experience, while not unique, became increasingly rare by 1870, when notaries claimed a much more central role in tying non-related lenders and borrowers together.

Families and the reliance on kinship networks are a central story line in Yucatán's history. The weight of the families and networks that made up the Casta Divina overshadows many interpretations of the henequen boom. But in the context of this closer analysis of kinship and the mechanics of trust in mortgage contracts, the extended connections between the notary and people outside easily recognizable family networks may have been more instrumental than a family connection. Notaries created trust, and thereby provided a very strong institutional tie, one that could trump family ties, suggesting that the historical development of Mérida's credit networks and capital flows relied less on the political hierarchy of family networks than on the market-oriented hierarchy of risk.

Mérida might have been a small and lively provincial city in the mid-1800s, but even casual acquaintance among its inhabitants did not prevent elements of asymmetric information to prevail in the interaction between lenders, borrowers, and their notaries. Asymmetric information signifies that not all parties to an agreement will have the same information about one another and that this unequal information will lead to an imbalance of power. This imbalance can be at least partly resolved by intermediation, which makes up for the unequal disclosure of information created by the asymmetry.

A lender and a borrower who agreed to a contract still had basic conflicting interests. The lender's need to be repaid and to reduce the risk of not being repaid may have been in exact opposition to the borrower's need to get a loan and hide a history of bad debts or the existence of prior and outstanding loans. The lender's need for information about a borrower and the borrower's need to withhold details would have been the essence of asymmetric information in Yucatán's credit market, a problem the notary would help resolve.

Similarly, the borrower may have wished to reveal positive aspects of the credit history or the quality of the collateral, which the lender may not have had access to or may have disbelieved. Notaries could bridge the information gap and balance out the asymmetries caused by this limited knowledge. This intermediary function was not a formal part of the notary's profession, but it was in this secondary and informal role that the notary played the most important part in Yucatán's nineteenth-century personal credit economy. This function developed as a consequence of the structural changes in the economy brought on by the henequen boom and by the formal changes in the legal environment.

In the early part of the 1850s and 1860s, the problem of asymmetric information was not an obvious one. Economic activity was restrained, the population level was relatively stable, and ecclesiastical lenders still dominated the market. In this context, defaulting on an obligation to an ecclesiastical institution carried with it not only the threat of future difficulties in accessing church funds but also the potentially more damaging risk of offending the church or a priest. Furthermore, few mortgage loans were being made, because neither the economic nor the legal context provided much of an incentive to the credit market.

By 1870 these kin ties and ecclesiastical privileges in the credit market had been all but eradicated. Relative political stability following the Caste War contributed to rising population levels through the end of the century, as workers from neighboring states moved to work on Yucatán's plantations.[23] In the mortgage market, average loan contracts became increasingly large, and the cost of borrowing rose as well, growing from below 6 percent per year in the 1850s and 1860s to well above 10 percent per year in the latter decades of the century. Formalization of the notarial codes and the elimination of the definition of usury in the civil codes allowed notarial loan contracts to represent the entire range of securitized credit transactions, and as a result, what little kinship lending there was all but disappeared. Lenders became a disparate group of lending individuals, not institutions.

Even so, it remained a small market, and small markets tend to be concentrated; small, emerging markets, such as Yucatán's, tend to be even more so because of the risk involved in developing new ventures. In these contexts, investors usually required greater guarantees of security before exposing their capital to risk. While the concentration of information, wealth, and power has negative effects in the long-term, in nineteenth-century Mérida it behooved lenders and borrowers to transact with those they knew and trusted. So as the economy grew and the need for lenders and borrowers spilled beyond the networks provided by kin, the information obstacles and problems inherent in credit transactions grew as well, and notaries stepped in to offer a potential solution.

The Mechanics of Intermediation

Information remained the notary's main asset, and it was also the most important currency in his client interactions, such as those dealing with wills and guardianships, a staple of a notary's daily business and a large part of his ledgers. Notaries also recorded land sales and mortgages, which were more subject to the vagaries of the economy. Land and real estate sales provided notaries with significant amounts of information about their clients and their potential client base—information that was central to their relationship with lenders and borrowers and that was supported by the large number of these sales they recorded. As fig. 4.1 illustrates, notaries always recorded more sales than mortgages. The figure illustrates the number of sales contracts and mortgage contracts recorded by the Mérida notaries between 1860 and 1890.

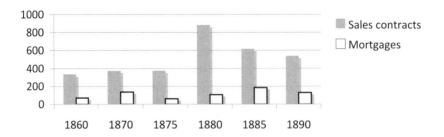

Fig. 4.1 Sales and mortgage contracts in notarial ledgers
SOURCE: Protocolos notariales, AGEY and ANEY.

The sales data was recorded using the indices at the beginning or the back of ledgers and reinforces the role of previous and repeated interactions as a powerful source of information for notaries and a key piece in the mechanics of the information flow that the notary controlled.

Mortgage contracts can be opaque documents that say little about what happened before the contract was written. But we can read from the trends in the contracts that no matter where or how lenders and borrowers came into contact with each other, the lender chose which notary recorded the transaction. The evidence suggests that lenders and borrowers developed very different relationships with the notaries based on diverse needs. Clients chose their notary when they lent, but if these clients needed to borrow, they would have to follow their lender to the notary of his or her choosing. And while most lenders transacted exclusively with one notary, other lenders recorded their loans with a different notary for each transaction.

Similarly, some borrowers appeared repeatedly in a notary's ledger, but most borrowers appeared only once during 1850–1900, and therefore only once in any of the notaries' ledgers. The borrowers who engaged in repeat business, however, tended to transact with one notary over successive transactions. The notary's relationship with his clients, especially those who looked to borrow repeatedly, created an incentive for borrowers to return to the same notary's office in search of potential lenders, which also promoted good behavior among borrowers who might want to be put in contact with lenders.

Lenders also benefited implicitly from dealing with one notary (or very few). The ledgers of a notary maintained the history of the lenders' transactions, and thus staying with the same notary minimized the bureaucratic side of any transactions. Furthermore, the notary's knowledge about his client base (especially those clients who might borrow) influenced the notary's ability to steer a lender to one borrower over another. This ability and the skill with which it was exercised were at the heart of the mechanics of the mortgage market during this period. As one notary's market share increased, so did the quality of his information about clients, and the better the information about potential borrowers, the greater the tendency among lenders to record credit transactions solely with that notary's office.

The differences of the notary's relationship with lenders as compared with his relationship with borrowers become more apparent if we analyze repeated interactions. Focusing on those who lent or borrowed more than once during 1850–1900 reveals patterns in their behavior that point to the logic of the notarial role in the mortgage market, as well as the logic of lenders' and borrowers' behavior.

For the purpose of clarity, clients who interacted repeatedly with one notary are referred to as "loyal," a term that suggests a measure of constancy in the relationship.[24] Similarly, clients who recorded their mortgage transactions with different notaries over time are called "switchers." This nominal distinction between loyal clients and switchers, especially after considering whether the clients were borrowers or lenders, reveals patterns of individual behavior as well as insight into the role of notaries.

NOTARIES AND REPEAT LENDERS   In any economy, lenders have a privileged position: they have what everyone, especially borrowers, want. Growth requires investment, and in a cash-strapped economy, those with resources are the fortunate ones. But resources are wasted if they are not put to productive use, and lenders in Mérida had to be judicious. Much has been written on the ostentatious consumption of wealthy henequen *hacendados*, but these comments are usually a criticism of the marble palaces and elegant homes built at the turn of the twentieth century in Mérida and the opulent haciendas of the henequen zone. We know little about the effect of this consumption on urban employment rates and infrastructure development. Regardless, at the onset of the henequen boom and throughout the nineteenth century, notarial credit contracts revealed a concern among lenders to allocate their wealth profitably. Once Benito Juárez lifted the interest-rate restrictions imposed by usury laws, most mortgage loans carried an interest rate, revealing the nonaltruistic nature of a credit market. Just as lenders loaned their money for profit, they wanted guarantees that profits would indeed materialize. While covenants built into credit contracts were part of this guarantee, the bond of lender and notary and the extended relationship notaries had with other parties and offices enhanced a lender's sense of security.

The data set of mortgages reconstructed for this study reveals three types of lenders: (1) those who lent only once; (2) those who lent more than once, each time using the same notary; and (3) those who lent more than once but recorded these contracts with different notaries. Because the relationship between a lender and a notary was affected by the number of times they worked together, one-time lenders cannot tell us much about repeat interactions. Loyal lenders loaned more than once with usually just one notary to record their loans, and switchers lent more than once in any year but not necessarily using the same notary.[25]

The analysis here of repeat lenders and notaries spans fifty years, during which time some notaries left the profession because they died or retired. That said, what determined a lender's repeated visits to the same notary's office? Proximity to their residence would be a likely explanation, but most notaries practiced in the city center, close to the main square, so they would all have been equally near or far from any other part of town. Simple force of habit may also provide an explanation, but that only tautologically explains what drove the habit in the first case. Furthermore, if loyalty were a force of habit, there would be no reason to see rates of loyalty change over time as we see it happening in Mérida. Nevertheless, habits have a way of reinforcing themselves, and if we consider the rate at which notaries recorded *other* contracts (that were not mortgages), we begin to see how some notaries would become more valued by lenders in the mortgage world than others.

Table 4.5 approaches this quandary. Habit alone was not enough to sustain a long-term relationship with one notary; loyalty resulted from a notary's ability to feed the relationship with information about potential borrowers, guaranteeing better security for the lender. Lenders became increasingly loyal to their preferred notaries (see column 3), especially after 1880, when more than half of all loans were issued by repeat lenders (see column 1). Columns 4 and 5 show the results, respectively, of the average number of contracts by lenders who switched notaries and the average number of contracts by lenders who remained with the same notary. Starting in 1885, around two-thirds of lenders continued working with the same notary.

Among the mortgages sampled, loyalty proportions were generally low before the henequen boom. The year 1860 stands out as a time when loyal lenders represented 71 percent of total repeat business that year (column 3),

Table 4.5 Repeat lenders and lender loyalty

	1 Percentage of contracts by repeat lenders[a]	2 Rate of switching by repeat lenders (%)[b]	3 Rate of loyalty by repeat lenders (%)[c]	4 Contracts per average switching lender	5 Contracts per average loyal lender	6 Total contracts in year
1850	37.14	80.77	19.23	3.50	2.50	70
1860	30.88	28.57	71.43	2.00	2.25	68
1870	45.19	62.30	37.70	4.75	3.83	135
1875	25.86	73.33	26.67	2.20	2.00	58
1880	50.98	65.38	34.62	3.09	2.43	103
1885	55.43	35.29	64.71	3.27	3.30	184
1890	47.29	36.07	63.93	3.14	2.79	129
1895	53.15	33.90	66.10	3.33	3.89	111

SOURCE: Protocolos notariales, AGEY and ANEY.

NOTE: "Repeat lender" refers to a lender who transacted more than once in that given year. It does not account for repeat lending through the years.

[a] The number of contracts by repeat lenders is divided by the total number of contracts.
[b] The number of contracts by switching lenders is divided by the total number of contracts by repeat lenders.
[c] The number of contracts by loyal lenders is divided by the total number of contracts by repeat lenders.

although the total number of contracts by these loyal lenders—sixteen—was quite low. Also, the analysis of loyalty in the period prior to the final alienation of ecclesiastical wealth in Yucatán has to consider the weight of ecclesiastical lenders before 1860.[26] Public welfare institutions, such as the Instituto Literario and the Hospital General, took over debts from different ecclesiastical funds and through 1875 continued to administer the credit contracts alienated from the church. Their share of total loans accounts for the seemingly high rates of loyalty among lenders in the early period of analysis, especially because institutional lenders accounted for up to one-third of total loans in 1860. As of 1875, however, the share of institutional loans had dwindled, and credit through individual lenders became the norm.

The trend in column 3 shows that loyalty levels increased in the latter part of the century. In 1895, 53 percent of lenders were repeat lenders (see column 1), and of these, two-thirds were loyal to the same notary (see column 3), making it the year with the highest proportion of loyal lenders except for 1860. Furthermore, loyal lenders consistently accounted for more than 50 percent of repeat lenders after 1880. Column 4 shows that switchers lent on average at least three times a year, except in 1860 and 1875, when they lent only twice. Loyalty was important and it created a fertile relationship among notaries and their clients, but it was not essential to the market. Loyalty increased, but switching lenders were named in two to three contracts per year.

As economic activity (including sales transactions, as seen in table 4.5) increased, lenders extended loans to many borrowers, and repeat lenders tended to concentrate most of their credit activity in one notarial office. Table 4.6 shows the distribution of loans by size among loyal lenders and switchers and illustrates differences in their lending behavior. As the total peso amount of credit contracts increased between 1850 and 1895, especially after 1880, the percentage of pesos lent by loyal lenders generally increased as well. In this changing economic context, stability in a lender's relationship with an intermediary such as a notary provided a measure of security and reinforced the ties between the two. Repeat lending did not mean, however, that larger amounts were lent per contract (until 1890), as column 2 points out. Table 4.6 further analyzes the distribution of contracts among repeat and loyal lenders and assesses this distribution by the total value of loans, rather than by the number of contracts as shown in table 4.5. Increasing numbers of mortgages were being lent repeatedly by the same group, but this trend did not result in larger average amounts per

Table 4.6 Size and distribution of credit contracts by repeat and loyal lenders (pesos)

| | 1 | 2 | 3 | 4 | 5 | 6 |
	Total lent in year	Amount lent by all repeat lenders	Amount lent by loyal lenders	Percentage lent by repeat lenders	Percentage lent by loyal lenders	Loyal loans divided by repeat loans (%)
1850						
Total	74,158	29,826	11,421	40.22	15.40	32.29
Average	1,091	1,147	1,903			
Median	525	802	422			
1860						
Total	84,002	15,318	12,318	18.24	14.66	80.42
Average	1,235	858	725			
Median	965	600	500			
1870						
Total	192,365	72,249	26,960	37.56	14.01	37.32
Average	1,436	1,165	999			
Median	650	700	721			
1875						
Total	156,667	64,967	44,500	41.47	28.40	68.50
Average	2,749	4,060	11,125			
Median	1,000	1,000	11,750			
1880						
Total	268,752	100,195	47,845	37.28	17.80	47.75
Average	2,635	1,890	1,543			
Median	1,450	1,000	1,015			
1885						
Total	751,426	310,097	217,927	41.26	29.00	70.28
Average	4,048	2,352	2,090			
Median	1,200	650	250			
1890						
Total	937,309	256,100	197,700	27.32	21.09	77.20
Average	6,601	4,341	4,822			
Median	2,000	2,000	1,900			
1895						
Total	894,402	475,800	377,200	53.20	42.17	79.28
Average	7,915	8,651	8,573			
Median	3,000	3,000	3,750			

SOURCE: Protocolos notariales, AGEY and ANEY.

mortgage. The amounts being lent per mortgage varied between the lender categories, and the average-size loan by a loyal lender exceeded the average only in three of the eight periods. In 1895 the average loan amount by loyal lenders was slightly higher than the total average, and it was very close to the average amount for repeat lenders; 1875 is an outlier year with two loans for twenty thousand pesos each by Victoriano Nieves, a loyal lender (and henequen trader), offsetting the balance. The averages and medians of repeat lenders compared to the averages of loyal lenders (columns 2 and 3) were similar enough (except in 1875, which is thrown off by one large contract) to suggest that loyalty or repeat activity did not affect the size of the loans.

Column 2 shows the sums lent by all the repeat lenders who lent more than once in a year. Column 3 shows the total amounts lent by those lenders loyal to one notary in the given year. Columns 4 and 5 calculate the percentage of total loans by repeat and loyal lenders.[27] Column 6 reveals a significant trend within the boundaries of this measure—loyal lenders became increasingly important in the market (but there were always more loans by repeat lenders than by loyal lenders). In the years after 1870, loyal lenders generally made more than 50 percent of the peso loans made by repeat lenders. Lenders who made more loans and lent larger amounts increasingly relied on the services of a single notary, thus supporting the hypothesis that the more transactions a lender entered into, the more the lender relied on one notary. This further supports the anecdotal cases, which show that the increasing market share of one notary accompanied the increasing reliance of prolific repeat lenders on that leading notary.

The development of this type of loyalty indicated growing trust between client and notary. These bonds were reinforced by the personal relationships that were the backbone of social interactions, especially when the rewards were positive. Personal relationships and word-of-mouth mechanisms undoubtedly helped notaries develop their reputation in the city and with their clientele, and in this market, where financial information relied on informal means of delivery, the notary was in a privileged position to receive and selectively distribute information to and about his clients.

In this context, loyalty to notaries became associated with their market share, leading the rate of loyalty to become associated with high levels of concentration of notarial activity in the mortgage market. Table 4.7 illustrates the concentration levels in the mortgage market. It accounts only for notaries who at some point between 1850 and 1895 recorded at least 20 percent of all credit contracts. The table traces the growth of their share before and sometimes after they reach this level and, of course, ignores notaries who never recorded that many mortgages.

In every year, two notaries usually recorded more than 50 percent of all private mortgages. In doing so, they contributed to the increasing central-

Table 4.7 Concentration and market share among Mérida notaries (%)

	1850	1860	1870	1875	1880	1885	1890	1895
Manuel Barbosa	3.74	**27.18**	7.44	3.28	—	—	—	—
Pedro José Canto	2.40	—	—		—	—	—	—
Manuel de la Calleja	2.67	—	—		—	—	—	—
Francisco del Río	8.35	9.06	—		—	—	—	—
Manuel Fernández	7.19	—	—		—	—	—	—
Pedro Irabien	0.69	—	—		—	—	—	—
Joaquín María Mendoza	0.96	4.99	—		—	—	—	—
Antonio Patrón	**22.91**	—	—		—	—	—	—
Eugenio del Rosario Patrón	**29.39**	—	—		—	—	—	—
Gumersindo Poveda	1.74	—	—		—	—	—	—
José Dolores Rocha	**19.96**	—	—		—	—	—	—
Ladislao Cantón	—	17.54	—		—	—	—	—
José Anacleto Castillo	—	13.1	20.26		—	7.49	0.27	—
Manuel Ávila Maldonado	—	20.54	9.04	**23.77**	8.93	—	**13.93**	8.72
José María Río	—	7.57	3.61	—	—	—	—	—
Francisco Flota	—	—	**37.79**	**42.26**	**47.66**	—	0.57	—

(continues)

Table 4.7 (continued)

	1850	1860	1870	1875	1880	1885	1890	1895
Francisco Rojas	—	—	**29.35**	1.48	0.19	—	—	—
Tomás Ruiz	—	—	1.24	—	—	—	—	—
José Ceferino Aguilar	—	—	5.79	—	—	—	—	—
José Antonio Alayón	—	—	5.48	—	—	—	—	—
Carlos Aranda	—	—	—	6.89	**25.56**	**14.36**	—	—
Eligio Guzmán	—	—	—	**17.91**	—	5.71	—	—
José Anacleto Patrón Zavalegui	—	—	—	3.16	11.36	**30.70**	**71.29**	**78.95**
José María Sánchez	—	—	—	1.25	1.45	9.64	10.51	—
Tomás Aranda Arceo	—	—	—	—	3.40	—	—	—
José Dolores Torres Aranda	—	—	—	—	1.45	0.21	—	—
José Andrade	—	—	—	—	—	**27.03**	0.47	3.73
Gregorio Pérez Escarrega	—	—	—	—	—	4.86	2.29	0.74
Miguel Acevedo	—	—	—	—	—	—	0.02	—
José Antonio Alayón	—	—	—	—	—	—	0.65	—
Avelino López	—	—	—	—	—	—	—	0.18
Alfonso Peniche	—	—	—	—	—	—	—	7.68
Total amounts transacted (pesos)	74,482	84,002	192,865	272,786	268,752	130,077	907,054	1,092,038

SOURCE: Protocolos notariales, AGEY and ANEY.

ization of the mortgage market in the late nineteenth century, and table 4.7 shows that it had always been so. Unlike their French counterparts, the notaries of Mérida did not share equally and instead had always vied for greater shares of the private mortgage market. In Mérida, private credit relied on a few key notaries rather than on all of them equally.[28] From 1860 to 1880, two notaries handled at least 40 percent of the recording of mortgages. In 1860 Manuel Barbosa and Ávila Maldonado had more than 45 percent of the market between them, and in 1870 Francisco Flota and Francisco Rojas handled close to 70 percent of the credit contracts. Between 1875 and 1880 Flota led, with Carlos Aranda and Eligio Guzmán far behind. As of 1885 Patrón Zavalegui rose to prominence and his share of the market would outweigh any other notary's through the end of the century.

LENDER LOYALTY   The previous analysis accounts for the behavior of repeat lenders, but it cannot account for lenders and the relationships they had with notaries with whom they transacted over many years. Notarial market share rather than loyalty emerges as an important binding mechanism between lenders and notaries, and therefore the behavior of some individual lenders over time (rather than in a single year) better illustrates how these mechanisms overlapped. The following example of just this type of long-term relationship is the kind that tied lenders to their favorite notary.

In 1885 Manuel Zapata Bolio lent Mex$10,000 to Miguel Peón (one of the members of the extensive Peón family) through the notary José Andrade in the only recorded loan Zapata Bolio made that year. Then in 1890 he lent Mex$600 to Josefa Espinosa de Navarrete, this time through Patrón Zavalegui. (Another member of the Mérida elite, Espinosa de Navarrete was on the committee that would plan the entertainment for Mexico's first lady during Porfirio Díaz's visit to Yucatán in 1906.)[29] In 1895 Zapata Bolio made nine loans for a total of Mex$137,000, all of which were signed by Patrón Zavalegui and amounted to almost one-fifth of the total allocated through the notary's office that year. Another lender who became a loyal Patrón Zavalegui client was Manuel Dondé Preciat. He made only one loan in 1875 through notary Ávila Maldonado, and in 1880 made another loan through notary Flota. Between 1885 and 1895, all the loans he made went through the office of Patrón Zavalegui, with the exception of one contract in 1890. All of these lenders were also loyal in using their preferred notary for other transactions, and it is in these repeated interactions, highlighted by their recurrent use of one notary to record the loans they made, that the importance of trust in the intermediary unfolds. The connection between lenders and notary was not kinship based, but it was foundational.

NOTARIES AND BORROWERS   Potential borrowers who did not have access to lenders had to acquire the trust of the notary first, and borrowers who mortgaged their properties to raise funds usually preceded this by interacting closely with one notary. Bibiano Aguilar, for example, borrowed in 1890 and 1895 only through the office of Patrón Zavalegui. Each of his loans was from a different lender, using different collateral in his small hometown of Conkal (about ten miles east of Mérida). Aguilar was a trader and his main residence was in Mérida, but he owned property in his hometown. In the first recorded mortgage, he borrowed from a well-known Mérida trading-house owner, Eusebio Escalante Bates; the subsequent loans were through local Conkal residents.[30] Aguilar's occupation is significant because it confirms a trend in the Yucatán credit market: borrowers who were linked to henequen most often borrowed from lenders who were also involved in the production and trade of henequen.

Another measure of constancy in the borrowing pattern was that repeat borrowers ended up borrowing through the same notary every time, although most of them in the data set did it only once. Any conclusions about borrower behavior must take into consideration that repeat borrowers were a small portion of total borrowers. Their proportion among borrowers over time did not change in a systematic way, and it was actually slightly lower in 1895 (14 percent) than in 1850 (when 24 percent of borrowers were repeat borrowers).[31] Borrowers rarely borrowed more than once a year (except in 1885, when a higher proportion borrowed a greater number of times), and when they did, they never borrowed from the same lender twice. So, while borrowing repeatedly was rare, it was accompanied by high rates of loyalty. Column 1 in table 4.8 illustrates this factor and shows the low rate of repeat borrowing, which is, however, matched in column 2 by extremely high levels of loyalty among these repeating borrowers, a loyalty that cemented their relationship with the notary. Column 3 accounts for the average number of loans in which repeating borrowers were named.

Table 4.8 shows that borrowers tended to follow lenders to the same notary in successive transactions and in doing so, as table 4.7 illustrates, increased the market share of a few notaries. Notaries who benefited from the rise in market share were profiting from the increasing concentration

Table 4.8 Repeat borrower and borrower loyalty

	1 Percentage of mortgages by repeat borrowers[a]	2 Percentage of mortgages by loyal borrowers[b]	3 Number of mortgages per repeat borrower	4 Total contracts in year
1850	24	50	2.29	70
1860	24	25	2.29	68
1870	23	52	1.94	135
1875	14	50	2.00	58
1880	28	66	2.07	103
1885	30	78	3.12	184
1890	20	100	2.08	129
1895	14	69	2.29	111

SOURCE: Protocolos notariales, AGEY and ANEY.

NOTE: Repeat borrowers may also be loyal borrowers, so columns 1 plus 2 may exceed 100 percent. A "repeat borrower" is a borrower who transacted more than once in a given year.

[a] The number of mortgages by repeat borrowers is divided by the total number of mortgages.
[b] The number of mortgages by loyal borrowers is divided by the total number of mortgages by repeat borrowers.

of information about their clients. Consequently, notaries became recipients of information about their borrowers (especially repeat borrowers), who benefited informally by having access to the notary's information about his other clients.

In an economic climate of high expectations and growth, information contained in the notarial ledgers, such as in the sales contracts, wills and testaments, and other documents attesting to a particular client's assets and reputation, became important, if not essential. The effect of this information chain fostered the relationships between potential borrowers and notaries who were known to have prolific client networks, and this tight connection then reinforced the relationship potential lenders might have with a notary, especially if they relied on him to provide information about a borrower's creditworthiness.

What this demonstrates is that the crucial, fundamental, and decisive relationship in the mortgage market was between borrower and notary, and not between lender and borrower. The success of the mortgage market was predicated on the fruitful outcome of the agreement between lender and borrower, but the notary was the crucial link between them. As table 4.8 shows, in every year except 1860, loyal borrowers accounted for at least 50 percent of repeat contracts. The notary helped borrowers gain access to lenders, and he was the constant element in the transactions, because none of these borrowers dealt with the same lender twice. In his daily and mundane dealings of recording wills or sales contracts, the notary garnered valuable information about his clients. The increasing loyalty of his clients implies that the centralization of activity among a few notaries contributed significantly to the agility of the market, especially if we think of this market as the space where lenders and borrowers interacted.

BORROWERS AND NETWORKS   Owning productive land or having the means to trade Yucatán's most profitable crop was, of course, crucial in order to borrow. Borrowers, especially those who remained loyal to one specific notary, also had identifiable stakes in the region's main agricultural activity. Fig. 4.2 illustrates how significant land (a proxy for henequen) and henequen trading was for borrowers in this credit market. The columns display the proportion of loans to all repeat borrowers who were landowners or traders versus the proportion of all mortgages lent to all borrowers not explicitly involved in henequen production or trade.

Fig. 4.2 is a graphic representation of what happens in small, concentrated, and growing markets. The economic momentum drives resources to the sector of the economy where its return is highest and most certain. In matters of credit, the bulk of the wealth generated by the henequen boom was lent to people involved in the trade or production of henequen. The graph is also a powerful illustration that the credit provided by the trading houses was not the only way to finance growth in the industry.

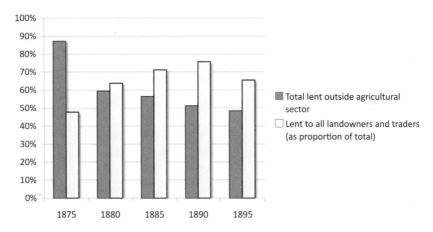

Fig. 4.2   Destination and use of loans
SOURCE: Protocolos notariales, AGEY and ANEY.

The share of loans to borrowers involved in henequen increased after 1875, even as other borrowers, such as cobblers or schoolteachers, obtained access to credit. The bulk of credit went to borrowers involved in the henequen economy, who not only had more valuable collateral (henequen or access to it) but also perhaps had greater need to raise capital for their commercial endeavors.

The henequen boom and the increasing value of agricultural land used for the production of henequen affected the mortgage market in a most obvious sense—henequen became a prized collateral commodity. In an environment rife with risk, henequen became a safe haven for creditors, who showed a growing preference toward borrowers with a connection to the henequen economy. As an increasing number of people devoted themselves in one way or another to this agricultural sector, their proportional part of the mortgage market increased. This trend is reflected in the occupations that borrowers stated in the contracts, where most of the borrowers identified themselves as traders and large landowners.[32] However, as the market turned more and more to agricultural borrowers, the occupational spectrum among borrowers widened. Cobblers, seamstresses, schoolteachers, and urban artisans also gained access to the credit market. Other merchants, such as butchers, fabric retailers, and a few clerical workers, also joined the ranks of the borrowers. However, among all these borrowers there was never a single repeat or loyal borrower who was a cobbler, a construction worker, a tobacconist, seamstress, or sorbet maker.[33] Perhaps not surprisingly, in this economy that now relied so much on henequen, borrowers who were not large landholders, henequen traders, or individuals that invested in henequen production remained a small component of this credit market.

Chapter Five

Credit the Wife
Marital Property Regimes and Credit Markets

In Mérida of Yucatán, on the tenth day of February of the year one
thousand eight hundred and ninety-one. Appearing before me, José Andrade,
notary public of the State, and witnesses who will sign, Mr. Don Lorenzo Peón,
forty-seven years of age, landowner, married to Mrs. Doña Cleta Cásares,
occupied in the labors of her gender, forty-seven years old, who agrees and
gives her consent to the validity of this instrument, both residents of this city,
and as they expressed and I faithfully know, Mr. Peón said that Mrs. Doña
Candelaria Escalante Duarte has conceded him the loan in the amount of
forty-five thousand pesos, which he will repay in the following way. . . .
—Extract of mortgage contract in ledger of notary José Andrade, 1891

Laws and property rights play an essential role in the functioning of credit
markets.[1] In the case of mortgages, which were by definition secured by
land, the credit market was determined by the structure of property rights,
including the mechanisms that determine how, within what parameters,
and by whom the asset can be used. Moreover, in credit markets, which
are an essential means of wealth distribution, the rights to use property, to
earn an income from property, and to sell it are all crucial. This is especially true in agricultural and preindustrial regions such as Yucatán in the
nineteenth century, where wealth was often in the form of real estate, effective ownership of it was central to the lending process, and real estate
should have putatively conferred access to credit. Yucatecan women were
active participants in the credit market, unlike Mayas, who were largely
absent from it. Both women and Mayas owned property, but among these
two minorities, only women appeared in the mortgage market. Women's
relationship to the most important conduit to credit, namely wealth, was
fraught with contradictions. It is in these contradictions that we may be

able to unearth the mechanism by which some property owners had access to credit markets, while others did not. The property rights of women were markedly different from those of men in the nineteenth century, and the institution of marriage profoundly affected these rights, with significant implications for the market and the women and men who participated in it.

This chapter analyzes marriage and the constraints it imposed on financial contracting. Marriage was a contract with historically significant financial corollaries, many of which were tied to property rights regimes, inheritance laws, and dowries—all designed to support the economic instrument that marriage represented. This chapter considers the effect of marriage on women in the Yucatán mortgage market.

Gender and Rights

Property rights determine access to and use of property, and in the nineteenth century, women's property rights also limited this access. Women were relatively active participants in the credit market of Mérida both as borrowers and lenders, but restrictions on married women's property rights resulted in distortions in the operation of the local credit market. These distortions and the central role that marital property regimes play present a prism though which to analyze and understand the effect of property rights on credit markets.

Mexican marital regimes could seem generous toward women, especially compared to Anglo-Saxon marriage laws. Mexican law preserved a separate legal personality for women and protected their right to own property in their own name. The marital regime also protected any property that belonged to a woman before she married and stipulated that premarital property remained hers throughout the marriage. The community property of the couple was the property acquired by either spouse during the marriage, and after death, the surviving spouse (husband or wife) received half of the community property, with the other half distributed among the rest of the estate heirs.[2]

The generosity of the Mexican codes had limits, however. While the Mexican marital property rights regime protected a wife's title to her property, it gave her husband exclusive power to administer his wife's property and use the community property by distinguishing between land title and land use. This scission between ownership and use damaged the seamlessness by which ownership should have conferred access to credit, and it affected married women especially. When a wife used her property as collateral on a loan, the constraints established by the law on the use and transfer of her property (as a married woman) tied her husband to the property and to the transaction.

This type of legal obstacle undermined the strength of a woman's property and transaction rights in Mexico, which in turn undermined women's participation in the credit market. This is not to say that women were not well represented in the Yucatán economy. On the contrary, as the henequen economy grew, growth in the credit market was largely supported by a small set of economic participants that included a significant number of women.[3] Women comprised 30 percent of lenders and 20 percent of borrowers between 1850 and 1895—a telling difference from women in the United States and Britain, who could not own assets and had to circumvent the coverture laws to achieve civil and economic independence.[4] Nevertheless, women in Mexico did not participate on an equal footing with their male counterparts, whether they were married or not. Compared with men, women paid on average two percentage points more interest.

The status of women in the law considered their innate weakness and provided them special protection in light of this assumption, and it distorted the conditions under which women lent and borrowed.[5] Women's property rights did not translate into rights of participation in the credit market. Barring quantitative value differences in the land female borrowers presented as collateral, the explanation to their unequal borrowing terms lies in qualitative assessments of the security of their collateral ownership. Gender, like ethnicity, was not in itself a barrier to ownership, but like ethnicity, it affected inclusion in the market.[6] The conditions under which Mexican women participated in nineteenth-century markets highlights how laws (and by extension, property rights and marital regimes) curtailed the formal rules of ownership and thereby increased the cost of ownership and credit.

Under Spanish colonial law, married women had a legal personality, and Roman law, from which the Latin American legal codes had sprung, provided an underlying recognition of women's property rights. The colonial pillars of legislation, the Siete Partidas and the Leyes de Toro, both focused on the aspects of private law regarding females, including their right to enter into contracts, their right to appear in court, and the scope of their husband's authority (if they were married) or their guardian's authority (if they were minors).[7] The Napoleonic Code, which inspired the independent Mexican legislators in the nineteenth century, continued the long tradition of securing these rights, especially for those individuals the state considered weak, such as women.

Mexico's first constitution as an independent country in 1824 granted citizenship to all Mexicans irrespective of property ownership or literacy, but the formal rights of women were limited (as was the case in many other countries at the time). The women of independent Mexico did not have the right to vote, married women continued to be subject to the will of their husbands in legal and economic matters, and widows were no more allowed to be guardians of their children's inheritance in 1824 than they had been under Spanish colonial law. The exclusion of women from this sphere of civil interaction "was considered so natural that it did not have to be specified in the constitution," and this treatment was not entirely out of line with the legal regimes in other parts of the world.[8]

Gender equality is a relatively recent civil prerogative, and in nineteenth-century Mexican law, rights, especially civil rights, depended on many variables, the first of which was gender. Mexico's nineteenth-century legal codes duly distributed property rights along these lines. Marital status was a unique variable in the distribution of rights among women, as only women were affected legally by a change in marital status, and unmarried women, including widows, could act with relative independence.[9] They could enter into transactions, manage their property, and appear in court without prior permission from a male. This independence was, of course, relative, because unmarried minors required guardians, and widows were not allowed to act as financial guardians to their children's wealth until the reform of the civil code in 1884. Similarly, underage widows returned to their underage civil status upon the death of their husbands. On the other hand, married women of any age had few civil liberties at all. Marriage returned women to a lesser civil status by subjecting them in many civil and economic matters to the will of their husband (as the Anglo-Saxon coverture laws did). Marriage did not eliminate a woman's rights absolutely: she held on to her legal persona, she could write a will (which covered her personal wealth, to which her husband had no rights of ownership), and she also shared in the joint property of the couple. Nevertheless, she could not initiate any other legal proceedings without the consent of her husband.

In the 1884 code, as in preceding ones, gender was the most obvious determinant of differences in the civil rights of women and men. Among women, age limits and marital status were the main barriers to legal equality. Even at the age of majority (twenty-five), the freedom to transact was conditional. After turning twenty-five, wives at any age required the express permission of their husbands before entering into a contract. Had they remained unmarried, women would eventually gain the right to transact individually upon turning thirty. A married woman never did, unless she became a widow.

This conditional age of majority remained in place until the 1884 Civil Code, enacted under President Porfirio Díaz, widened the scope of civil action for women. The new code did nothing to change the situation of married women, but it reaffirmed that a wife's freedom to transact was subject to the will of her husband. Wives continued to retain sole ownership of the assets they brought into the marriage, and husbands retained exclusive power to manage this property and have a final say in any contract she wished to sign. None of the nineteenth-century reforms changed the fact that marriage subjected women to the supervision and control of their husbands. Even if adult married women had a legal personality, marriage effectively limited the legal sphere in which they could act without their husband's consent. It was not until the death of her husband that a woman was liberated from almost all the legal shackles marriage had imposed on her, especially in the commercial context.

The laws afforded widows the widest legal berth, and widows were, in legal terms, most akin to men. There were some restrictions, however. If a widow remarried, she returned to a legally subordinate status, as a remarried widow was first and foremost a wife. If she was underage, she returned to the guardianship of her male parent. Until the enactment of the 1884 Civil Code, widows of any age were not allowed to act on behalf of their children because these minors required the guardianship of a man. The wealth their children inherited after the death of their father (her spouse) had to remain under the authority of either a male family member or an appointed male guardian. This changed after the 1884 reforms to the civil code, when widows and unmarried mothers (of legal age) were for the first time granted control over their children's inheritance.[10]

In Mérida, however, this change in the law did not make much of a difference. Before and after the passing of the 1884 law, widows who lent usually did so with their own money (the money they had brought into the marriage plus their half of the marital property over which they gained rights after the death of their husband, excluding the inheritance of their minor children), and they loaned money without the legal representation of a man. For example, in 1860 Fidelia Quijano de Lara lent two thousand pesos to María Encarnación Guzmán de Quijano. Both women were widows, and both signed on their own behalf, without the help of a male legal representative. Another widow, Concepción Troncoso, signed a mortgage in 1890, in which she lent her son Joaquin Duarte Troncoso thirty thousand pesos.[11] As widows, Concepción Troncoso and Fidelia Quijano represented a majority of the female lenders in Mérida, as well as a source of credit to enterprising Yucatecans looking for funds during the boom.

When these widows lent, they behaved very much as male lenders. They did not lend at lower or higher interest rates than men, they did not lend to a significantly different group of borrowers, and there were no specific differences in amounts lent or interest rates charged. In sum, there is nothing, save their gender and marital status, that differentiated these lenders from male lenders.[12] What is certain, however, is that among women, widows were the most prolific lenders, and that among widowed lenders (male or female), widows tended to transform most of their wealth into financial assets. Evidence from the probate records reveals the widows' particular preference for financial assets, far more than their male counterparts, who died with fewer outstanding credits and many more tangible assets. The probate records provide an inventory of the assets of the deceased, and although the sources have bias problems, they highlight an interesting practice among wealthy widows: Among the eleven widows who died with more than a thousand pesos in valued assets, five died with more than 50 percent of their assets lent out.[13]

When widows died, they left behind estates that were significantly larger than estates left behind by married or unmarried women, which explains why widows, who did most of the lending, might lend larger amounts than the married borrowers were borrowing. This tendency among widows to lend more than other women borrowed was not related to testamentary laws, since changes in testamentary freedom enacted under the 1884 Civil Code did not affect the testamentary traditions in Yucatán. Evidence from the probate records of the civil courts of Mérida reveal that spouses and children inherited and claimed property after 1884 under the same provisions as the previous code of 1870 and the Spanish codes of the colonial period.[14]

Candelaria Castillo de Villajuana's probate is illuminating because she was also one of the few women who lent before becoming a widow. Candelaria Castillo de Villajuana made some loans with the consent of her husband, Cosme Ángel Villajuana, a wealthy Mérida trader and civil judge. He was also a prolific lender, and when he died in 1895, the rights to half of the community assets that went to Candelaria included the loans owed her husband. Candelaria died in 1901, and the inventory of her assets, including the list of loans prepared in January 1895 during the probate of her husband's estate (some of which had been repaid by 1901), records more than Mex$70,000 in outstanding debts, representing more than 90 percent of the value of her entire estate.[15] Candelaria Villajuana's case was exceptional, and not all widows chose to lend so much of their wealth, but among those whose probate records survive, many did lend at least some small part of their wealth. As the probate documents show, the average wealth of widows at death was exponentially larger than the average wealth of wives or unmarried women, and this is a powerful explanation of their role as lenders in Yucatán.[16] They lent because they could.

Unmarried women, on the other hand, rarely lent or borrowed, even if they were legally entitled to do so after reaching adulthood. As minors, unmarried girls couldn't do anything with their wealth; only their guardians were allowed to lend and invest on their behalf, and when they came of age, they acquired the right to end the contracts drawn up in their name by a guardian. For instance, sixteen-year-old Mercedes Espinoza's father died in 1885, leaving her a small estate. Her grandfather, Miguel Espinoza Loza, became her guardian and lent Mex$1,820 of his granddaughter's inheritance to his other son, Mercedes's uncle. As her guardian, her grandfather signed his name at the bottom of the loan and initiated the procedures of the loan.[17] The loan did not determine a term date, but it clearly stipulated that Mercedes could call back the loan as soon as she became of age or any time thereafter (even if the record is unclear whether Mercedes ever recalled the loan).

Gertrudis Vado's history in the mortgage market is an example of unmarried women in the Mérida credit market. Gertrudis never married nor did she enter a convent or disappear into the opaque world of *labores domésticas*, the stated occupation noted next to her name. This term translates loosely into "domestic chores," a euphemism describing domestic tasks, specifically those that happened within the sphere of the personal home. The mortgage contracts she made at José Anacleto Patrón Zavalegui's office give us snapshots of the truly independent acts of Gertrudis, who was never accompanied by a guardian or a man when making the loans. According to the records of her notary, she lent at least twice in her adult life, first in 1875 at the age of twenty-five, when she lent Mex$1,800 for one year to Juan José Martinez, a hacienda owner, and then in 1885, when she lent another Mérida property owner, Joaquín Mangas, Mex$3,500 for three years. She charged the men 18 percent and 15 percent, respectively, per year, higher rates than average at the time.[18] In 1895 the records also show that Gertrudis borrowed Mex$3,000 for two years at an interest rate of 12 percent. This contract was recorded at the office of the notary Alfonso Peniche. The reasons why Gertrudis borrowed then at the age of forty-seven remain unknown but her previous loans show she was not a new-comer to this market, and perhaps it also explains why she paid slightly less than the average interest rate (the average interest for the six unmarried women who borrowed that year was 12.10 percent).

Women in the Credit Market

In the 1895 census in Mérida, the majority of the population was female (55 percent) and in the occupational breakdown, most of them were engaged in labores domésticas.[19] Among these housebound women were the wives, unmarried daughters, and widows who populated the mortgage market. The Mérida census accounts for a good number of women engaged in cleaning, cooking, and education; these women worked outside the family home and performed these tasks for a salary, in contrast to those focused on labores domésticas, which were not remunerated. The garment production industry employed most women outside the home, with almost a thousand women working either as seamstresses or fashion designers in 1895. Another seventeen hundred women were employed as cooks and cleaners. Other occupations that favored the employment of women were wet-nursing (Mérida had eight women in this understandably feminine profession), prostitution (seventeen), and midwives (twenty-four). Nevertheless, most women (60 percent) were not officially employed and probably spent most of their existence within the boundaries of the labores domésticas, the term itself reinforcing the separation of women from the public and commercial enterprises in which men were engaged.

This separation between the public and the private spheres, however, is not supported in the notarial evidence illustrated by table 5.1, which shows how intertwined women were in the public world of mortgage contracts. Women were, in fact, actively borrowing and lending between 1850 and 1895, even if the proportional amounts transacted by women were far outweighed by those transacted by men.

Table 5.1 illustrates the imbalance in the market—women lent more than they borrowed. As lenders, women represented a small group, but they

Table 5.1 Women in the mortgage market, Mérida

Borrowers	1 Amounts borrowed by women (pesos)	2 Women's share of total amounts borrowed (%)	3 Number of contracts to women borrowers	4 Women's share of contracts (%)	5 Average size of loans to women (pesos)	6 Average size of loans to men (pesos)
1850	14,414	19.35	14	20.59	1,030	1,112
1860	15,109	17.99	11	16.18	1,374	1,209
1870	25,834	13.39	36	26.67	718	1,687
1880	35,014	13.03	28	27.45	1,251	3,159
1890	86,800	9.57	33	25.58	2,630	8,544
1895	92,220	10.31	31	27.93	2,975	10,027

Lenders	Amounts lent by women (pesos)	Women's share of total amounts lent (%)	Number of contracts by women lenders	Women's share of contracts (%)	Average size of loans by women (pesos)	Average size of loans by men (pesos)
1850	18,017	24.19	17	25.00	1,060	1,107
1860	28,954	34.47	21	30.88	1,379	1,171
1870	23,021	11.94	17	12.59	1,354	1,439
1880	39,528	14.71	16	15.69	2,471	2,665
1890	158,505	17.47	25	19.38	6,340	7,198
1895	145,938	16.32	29	26.13	5,032	9,128

SOURCE: Protocolos notariales, AGEY and ANEY.

could make relatively large contributions to the total of loans in any year, which is mostly explained by the fact that female lenders were usually widows—a select and, by definition, wealthier group.[20] The second column in table 5.1 aggregates the amounts women were borrowing and lending in this market, and columns 5 and 6 illustrate the difference in average loan sizes between women and men. Once again, the unequal effect of the economic boom is illustrated in the relative growth in average loan sizes. In 1850 and 1860 women and men borrowed and lent comparable average amounts per mortgage contract, but at the time of the transition to large-scale henequen manufacturing in the 1870s, the average size of loans to men increased significantly. The average size of loans *by* women, except in 1895, barely differs from that of men because female lenders were widows, with significantly expanded property rights compared to their married counterparts. Female borrowers on the other hand were mostly married women.

The participation of all these women, both as lenders and as borrowers, provides a glimpse into an oft-overlooked reality about the participation of women in mundane financial affairs. Research on the economic activity of women is much more complete for the colonial period and the twentieth century, but we know relatively little about how women, especially elite women, used the money and assets the law entitled them to own in the nineteenth century.[21] The table cannot reflect what the loans were being used for, but it does show that in the nineteenth century, women in Yucatán were active participants in the credit market and that the constraints to women participating in elite commercial circuits were not absolute.

Table 5.2 succinctly illustrates one of the most interesting aspects of women's presence in the Yucatán credit market, namely the disparity between the interest rates charged to men and women over time.[22] The most onerous aspect of this participation and a consequence of the legal differences between men and women, especially as borrowers, is that women paid on average up to two percentage points more than men. The disparity charted in the table is not a statistical accident—it is a very robust statistical reality.[23]

Mexico's laws conferred different legal capacities to adult women according to their marital status, defining them as "widowed," "married," or "unmarried." Using these categories to reanalyze the interest-rate evidence, we see that marriage, more than any other variable, affected interest rates. The evidence suggests that women paid a penalty in credit markets

Table 5.2   Average interest rates by gender of borrower (number of contracts in parentheses)

	Women (%)	Men (%)	Difference
1880	11.43 (28)	9.80 (74)	1.63
1885	14.69 (29)	11.85 (155)	2.84
1890	13.61 (32)	12.08 (107)	1.53
1895	11.54 (31)	11.19 (80)	0.35

Source: Protocolos notariales, AGEY and ANEY.

and it was, by any measure, a marriage penalty. Results from regression analyses showed that the length of the loan did not affect the interest rate. The location of the collateral affected interest, but this was a common trait among all borrowers. Marital status, on the other hand, was statistically significant for women only. The positive coefficient estimates the penalty at more than 2 percent. These results and the interest-rate penalty they highlight are reinforced by the fact that in most years, except for 1895, the majority of women borrowers were, in fact, married women. Therefore, the borrowing premium reflected not only the marriage penalty, but the fact that most of the borrowers were married, as table 5.3 illustrates.

Married women borrowed often; widows and unmarried women rarely did. Not only did married women borrow more and pay more than any other women, they also outnumbered the other two groups. Of the twenty-eight female borrowers in 1880, 61 percent were married. In 1885, 55 percent of the twenty-nine female borrowers were married. In 1890 and 1895, about half of the female borrowers were married (eighteen of thirty-two in 1890 and fifteen of thirty-one in 1895).

Table 5.3   Average interest rates by marital status and gender (number of contracts in parentheses)

	Average interest rates to unmarried women	Average interest rates to widowed women	Average interest rates to married women	Average interest rates to male borrowers	Average interest rates to all borrowers	Proportion of contracts by women (%)
1880	12.60 (5)	9.30 (6)	12.40 (17)	9.80	10.60	27
1885	15.80 (5)	17.60 (8)	19.20 (16)	11.85	15.90	28
1890	13.80 (7)	15.00 (7)	14.30 (18)	12.08	12.50	23
1895	12.10 (6)	11.60 (10)	13.20 (15)	11.19	11.40	27

Source: Protocolos notariales, AGEY and ANEY.

Interest rates in loans reflected the risk embodied in each borrower, and there were a myriad of unobservable reasons why anyone would pay higher rates. Generally, the availability of information about a borrower was a crucial element in risk assessment and determining interest rates. Another element relied on information about the context in which the loan was to be made and the external conditions that would make repayment possible or not.

Most lenders assessed risk based on what they knew about the borrowers. Previous interactions with a borrower or someone close to the borrower (such as a notary) provided information such as a track record as a bad payer, a reputation as a gambler, or the challenge of an ailing business—all of which would lead to higher interest rates. Alternatively, positive previous interactions or recommendations from trusted colleagues (or again notaries) could help reduce the interest rate. But when there was no information or very little information about a borrower, a lender had to assume the worst and estimate an interest rate that could protect against a perceived risk. The risk inherent in any loan was a product of combining real and perceived risks.[24]

In this assessment of risk, a lender needed to consider the possibility that women, especially married women with children, might receive more lenient treatment from the legal system. The colonial laws had protected women from destitution and abuse, especially concerning their dowries, and while the protection was meant to secure the integrity of the family estate, the justifications for it that survived into the nineteenth century were based on notions of innate feminine weakness. These legal biases could have represented a real risk for any lender, especially if creditors feared the courts might favor women in first-order lines of repayment if they were lenders or be more forgiving if they were borrowers. While the courts could avail themselves of the right to distribute an estate to the surviving wife and children ahead of creditors, there is absolutely no evidence in Yucatán that the courts intended to or ever did privilege delinquent female debtors.

If borrowing women did not present this type of risk to lenders, it still leaves us with an unknown: why did married women pay higher interest rates than widows or women who never married? Did married women constitute a greater credit risk? Was it simply a perceived risk by virtue of their absence from the traditionally male centers of commercial and financial activity? All women, irrespective of marital status, and especially among the elite and urban middle class, were largely left out of the commercial circle of Yucatán's masculine world of henequen trade. Their interaction was limited as wives and mothers of landowning hacendados and daughters of traders, but the day-to-day business was not theirs. Women held wealth (through dowries, inheritances, and community property partitions), and they were not entirely removed from the commercial world, but their world was constrained by the domestic nature of the circles in which they moved, while trade and finance generally happened between men. The persistent interest-rate difference between married women and other borrowers suggests that interest rates, with their built-in assessment of risk, hinged not just on women's limited exposure to the commercial market and its social distinctions, but also on characteristics of married women relative to their property rights status.

The correlation between marital status and interest rates was not just a random coincidence, but it cannot account for the causality that drives this relationship, and an explanation of the logic of the relationship between marriage and the cost of borrowing for women lies in the legal texts. The centrality of property rights in the assessment of credit risk is at the core of the interest-rate differential that married women experienced in the mortgage market.

The Predicament of Marriage

Widows were once wives, but beyond this, the similarity ends. Compared with widows in the mortgage market, wives with living husbands were more likely to be borrowers, to borrow higher amounts and more often, and to pay higher interest rates. The explanatory logic of these observations requires that we grasp them as different aspects of the same issue: married women were borrowing expressly because they were married. Marriage was an unequal partnership in which the husband had disproportionate rights over his wife, and in this relationship, when a woman borrowed, it was most likely because her husband requested she do so. By the same token, married women paid higher interest rates when they borrowed because of their husband; marriage connected women to husbands who represented a higher risk to lenders.

The reason men would have asked their wives to borrow on their behalf was simple: these men did it because they couldn't borrow on their own. The formal legal concept of *potestad marital* (literally translated as "marital power") gave the husband control over most aspects of his wife's life and property, but it didn't give him the right to use her property as collateral. If the husband wanted to use his wife's property as collateral, he had no choice but to allow her to initiate a loan.

Marital Power

Marriage altered the property rights of women through the concept and practice of potestad marital, which gave husbands tutelage and control over the wealth, time, and space of their wife.[25] Potestad marital was based on the notion that vesting authority in the husband alone would prevent antagonism between the spouses and maintain unity in the family and coherence in society. The diminished legal capacity of women was necessary to protect her economic and moral interests as the vulnerable sex, as well as to protect her husband and family.

Potestad marital originated in colonial legal codes and survived into the nineteenth century. As the legislators of independent Mexico waded through the mass of colonial laws governing civil affairs, they often returned to and relied on the Spanish colonial legal tradition for personal and family law. Nineteenth-century Mexican civil codes reflected the concerns of the Spanish codes, which enforced matrimonial peace by giving the husband the power to decide and maintain family unity, wealth, and social peace. Potestad marital afforded married women limited legal capacity; only when the husband was unable to perform his legal role (due to illness or old age, for example), could the wife step in. Barring this, husbands had complete control over the administration of the joint property of the couple, the wife's dowry, and her ancestral inheritance.[26] The husband's power further extended to the use of her time outside the home, specifically with respect to employment. The civil code also gave fathers authority over the children produced in marriage, as well as their inherited property. Until 1884, if any minors survived the father, a male guardian was appointed to administer the minors' inheritance until their marriage or adulthood.

Family law reflected a preoccupation among legislators with maintaining the integrity of family property. The system of equal inheritance was another pillar of the Mexican property regime, and it guaranteed women an inalienable right to their family's wealth. All children, irrespective of gender, inherited at least equal parts of the estate portion reserved for them, and this wealth could not be transferred or diluted through marriage. Parents did not have the right to disinherit their legal offspring, and although they could favor one at the expense of others, this favoritism was constrained by the law. Because parents could distribute only other parts of the estate to individual children, all siblings were at least guaranteed an income.[27] To ensure that the inheritors of a father's wealth were his biological children, there needed to be minimal doubt about the legitimacy of the offspring. The tutelage and laws controlling a wife's freedom in the marriage guaranteed to a degree that children of the marriage were the biological result of the union.[28] The genetic legitimacy of the child was supported by a guarantee of social legitimacy, which was assumed and accepted as long as a wife remained obedient in the eyes of society.

The way in which the legal restrictions were applied to women had ·much to do with the law's concern with women's biological ability to jeopardize the integrity of estates. As long as women were of childbearing age, the barriers were high. Once dilution of the family wealth through irresponsible procreation was less of a threat, the restrictions became less stringent. This explains the reduction of limitations on widows and long-term unmarried women, who would, by virtue of biology and the assumed celibacy of their status, be less likely to sire offspring of dubious origin.

Fig. 5.1 charts the age at which individual women, sorted by their marital status, lent or borrowed. As the figure illustrates, widows who lent (and sometimes borrowed) in Mérida were on average much older than married or yet unmarried women. The tutelage laws reflected the paternalistic prerogatives of the law and the biological function of the women it addressed. Laws and civil codes concerning women were designed to maintain the obedience of women within the family structure, which was both an economic unit and a pillar of social cohesion. The laws reflected the common concern among lawmakers that extending leniency and freedom to married women would put social and economic harmony at risk.

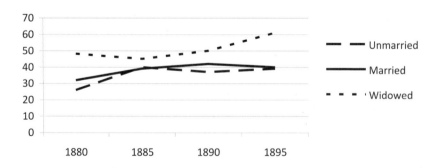

Fig. 5.1   Average age of women at time of contract
SOURCE: Protocolos notariales, AGEY and ANEY.

In this light, restricting the mobility and liberty of women, especially wives, was as much a fear of independent females, as it was a conservative concern with the safeguard of the family's estate. While the law protected a married woman's right to be the sole owner of her property, the law could not trust her to use this wealth.[29] Furthermore, since civil laws gave women rights to at least half of the family's assets, nineteenth-century lawmakers could not responsibly grant them the freedom to use this wealth, until it no longer posed a challenge to the power of the husband and a threat to the harmony of the family.

Because notaries were bound to record only contracts that were legal (under threat of severe penalties), it is highly unlikely that notaries recorded and oversaw contracts that went against the wishes of recalcitrant husbands.[30] The requirement that a wife defer to her husband's will was reinforced in the handbooks of instructions to Mexican notaries, which reiterated the restrictions on wives entering into contracts, especially those affecting her wealth (and by extension, the wealth of her children and her husband, were she to die first) or potentially involving a trial (either as a plaintiff or defendant) that could lead to public disgrace.[31] The notarial handbooks made no comments concerning unmarried women (unmarried girls who were still under the tutelage of their parents were strictly barred from contracting anyway). The reputation of women needed to be safeguarded at all costs, and this was best achieved if husbands were granted the widest possible discretion over their wives' transactions.

However, given all these proscriptions and obstacles to the participation of married women in the civil sphere, the evidence summarized in table 5.4 suggests that Yucatecan men often allowed their wives to borrow, yet rarely consented to them lending.

Table 5.4 Married women in the mortgage market, Mérida

	Number of borrowers	Number of lenders	Total amounts borrowed (pesos)	Total amounts lent (pesos)
1850	1	0	1,300	0
1860	5	2	10,209	1,200
1870	16	1	11,861	10,000
1875	10	3	12,111	4,300
1880	17	1	20,971	100
1885	26	8	38,970	17,200
1890	18	2	44,900	7,000
1895	15	8	25,450	12,700

SOURCE: Protocolos notariales, AGEY and ANEY.

In any year, borrowing wives far outnumbered lending wives. A married woman was far more likely to appear in this market to borrow than to lend both in terms of the number of contracts and amounts. Even in 1885, when married women lenders reached their peak in the sample, the amount they lent (seventeen thousand pesos) was less than half of what they borrowed (in excess of thirty-eight thousand pesos). Similarly, the number of married women who borrowed outnumbered those who lent in every year. Borrowing wives outnumbered the lenders by at least 100 percent (and nearly so in 1895); in 1870 and 1880, for example, only one wife lent and more than fifteen borrowed.

In light of the legal context discussed earlier, how do these figures contribute to our understanding of the interest-rate differential highlighted in table 5.2? How does this borrowing activity among married women relate to their borrowing costs? To answer these questions, we must consider the nature of the property being used as collateral in these loans. Notaries did not make explicit note of the property regime under which a collateralized piece of property belonged to an individual entering into a loan, but the signatures at the end of the loans by married parties, male and female, reveal its nature.

The signatures of spouses on mortgage contracts signified their approval of the contract, but not necessarily their shared liability in the debt. When marital property was used as collateral, then both spouses shared in the loss if the collateral was claimed as repayment. However, we cannot assume that the signature of a wife on her husband's loan contract was a sign that she was a coborrower. A wife's signature on the contract did not imply active participation in the credit market but instead reflected her knowledge and approval of a transaction involving communal property. Three-quarters of the loans by married male borrowers bore their wife's signature, suggesting that joint property was the main source of collateral. This also means that in the rest of the mortgages, the collateralized property was the sole property of the husband, and the contract did not require his wife to sign or be aware of anything happening to that property.

The inverse, however, was not true. When husbands signed at the end of a mortgage contract, as they inevitably did, they were not signaling their awareness and approval of a contract using joint property; they were signaling consent of a contract using property that was not theirs. After all, wives were not allowed to transact, let alone transact with communal property. They couldn't even manage their own property, never mind use joint property as collateral. Husbands did not sign as legal representatives or as guarantors (as was the case for fathers and substitute guardians signing on behalf of underage daughters and wards); they signed because without their signature, the notary could not legally record the contract, because it was illegal for any married woman to enter into any kind of contract without her husband's knowledge and approval.

The civil code further reinforced this one-way spousal control through article 1779. This article, which existed in the 1870 Civil Code and remained intact under the 1884 Civil Code, gave husbands the right to annul any contract signed by their wife without their express consent.[32] As per the code, husbands had this right during the marriage and retroactively for four years following the eventual dissolution of the marriage (either by divorce or death).[33] This article created an incentive for all parties to maintain the integrity of marriage, especially in economic terms. The laws protected the right to ownership for women, but article 1779 essentially destroyed the value of this property were she to use it as collateral in a contract without her husband's consent.

The situation was only slightly different among married lenders. In the rare cases when married women served as lenders, their husbands countersigned the contracts, indicating their knowledge and approval of the transaction. Husbands controlled their own property and the couple's communal property, but they had only administrative control, without any claims to ownership over their wife's property. Married women could transact only when using their own property, but the law gave the husband final say over his wife's decision to use this property.[34]

One notable legal exception allowed women to enter into contracts independently if they were acting in a commercial context. If women were engaged in a professional endeavor, the law presumed the agreement of the husband as long as the transaction was directly related to her stated profession.[35] Unfortunately, the mortgage contracts did not reveal much about the use of the loans, and the occupation stated in the contracts of most female lenders was always the rather limited definition of labores domésticas or de estado honesto (of honest standing). In the remaining cases, the occupation was either not stated at all or replaced by the general term of proprietaria (property owner), which was a testament to her wealth and social status rather than an occupational category.[36]

Mortgage contracts typically remained mute as to the purpose of the loan, but if women were actively using their borrowed funds to start up businesses, refinish the roof on their house, or plant new henequen seedlings, there is no reason why we should expect married women would do this more than unmarried or widowed women. If women were independently engaging in business or home-improvement projects, we would expect *all* women, irrespective of occupation or marital status, to borrow. Considering the restrictions the law imposed on married women in terms of their activities outside the house and their financial responsibilities within the household, we might even expect widows and unmarried women to borrow more than married women simply because they had greater legal freedom to do so. Instead, it was the women with the least control over their own property that borrowed the most.

This trend reinforces the relationship between marriage and the borrowing activity of women and implies that husbands were the causal mechanism that led married women to borrow more than other women. Furthermore, the marriage penalty that so clearly increased the interest rate for married women above all other borrowers can therefore be understood not simply as a function of laws protecting their gender or defining their marital status, but also as a function of their husbands.

Husbands as Market Obstacles

The interest-rate quandary posed at the beginning of this chapter has as much to do with the legal protections and restrictions toward women as it does with the ubiquitous shadow that followed wives into the notary's office. While the loans notaries recorded were initiated and signed by women using their own property as collateral, women were rarely the final users of the loan. The man sitting next to them across from the notary, the one who approved her use of the collateral to take out the loan, and the one who signed next to her name on the loan document was the most likely beneficiary of that transaction.

A wife could not legally borrow without the express consent of her husband, because independent use of her wealth constituted a threat to social and familial harmony. Her husband, in turn, could not use her assets without her collaboration, because the laws continued to protect ancestral property lines. In this arrangement, neither the wife nor the husband could legally act alone to effectively manage the wife's assets. While the husband had the right to administer his wife's assets, he did not have the right to sell, lend, or do anything else with them. If a husband needed to borrow for his own enterprises, he could use his wife's property as collateral only if she performed the transaction. Therefore, if a husband wanted to use his wife's property as security against a loan, his wife had to serve as the primary borrower. And for his wife to borrow, the husband had to grant her legal license to contract and then had to sign the contract as legal proof of his consent.

The connection between married women and the mortgage market was determined by husbands. Husbands explain both the interest-rate differential *and* the borrowing activity of married women. The marital partnership structured the loans in such a way that, while it seemed as if women were borrowing (they were, after all, signing the contracts and using their property as collateral), it was, in fact, the husband who originated the request for credit. Because a husband's rights over his wife did not extend to using her property as collateral for a personal loan, he would have had to use his privileged position as head of household and administrator of his wife's wealth to ask or gently pressure her to give him use of her property.

When a husband gave his wife the right to transact, he was giving her the right to use her property as collateral for a loan he would eventually use. Wives did not borrow for any specific projects they were involved in, because married women who borrowed were never employed outside the home. This evidence points to the husband as the true originator of the loan, where wives borrowed to raise funds for their husbands, meaning that loans to married women were, in fact, repackaged loans to husbands.

The reason why this resulted in higher-than-average interest rates is connected to the earlier discussion on the laws that controlled a wife's freedom to use her own wealth and restricted her husband's privilege over it as well. The world of commercial transactions was a masculine one, and even if widows were important lenders, most borrowers were men. These men, regardless of marital status, used their own assets to secure funds through the mortgage market, and they constituted the large share of borrowers and lenders in the credit market. They used either their own property or joint property to secure the loan, which not only conferred security to the mortgage, but also signaled to the lender that the borrower was solvent and the rightful owner of the bulk of his household's wealth.

On the other hand, husbands who granted their wife permission to transact sent a very different message to lenders. A husband's consent to let his wife use her property as collateral proved not only that the husband was not using his own assets but that he was probably dependent on his wife's wealth. Furthermore, there is no evidence among the mortgage contracts and a large sample of the sales contracts and land deeds recorded by notaries that these husbands owned any property at all, and their absence in the records constitutes the virtual evidence that the husbands of borrowing women had no assets of their own.[37] There are no surviving previous sales contracts or deeds that recorded any evidence of these men's assets, and in the case of these husbands, their name at the end of the contract generally constitutes the first and only evidence of their existence in the market.

In the absence of information about the history of most of these husbands, and the total lack of detail about the use of the loans made in the name of wives, there is one example, however, in the historical records that sheds light on the ways in which this mechanism might have unfolded. Blas Díaz, one of Mérida's sorbet makers, was married to forty-five-year old Antonia Pereira. In 1885 Antonia borrowed fifteen hundred pesos from Remigio Nicoli, a wealthy property owner in Mérida, and she put up as collateral her share of a house she owned with her sister, having inherited that home recently from their parents. For this transaction she paid 15 percent annual interest on the one-year loan. Five years later, Díaz borrowed three thousand pesos from another Mérida lender, putting up a house he now owned in Mérida as collateral. The couple no longer lived at the same address, and the henequen boom and Mérida's sweltering climate no doubt helped the sorbet business, because Díaz could now put up his own property as collateral, borrow in his own name, and pay 12 percent interest per year.[38]

Once Díaz no longer relied on his wife's property, he used his own property as collateral, and in this transaction, the interest rate was significantly lower than when his wife borrowed using her own property. The laws protecting women from repossession could not affect Díaz when he borrowed in his own name, and this was at least one of the reasons for his lower interest-rate cost. The other reason was that the lender was dealing directly with the borrower, as compared with the previous transaction, when the lender knew he was not just lending to Antonia but instead was financing a project that Díaz would control. In 1885 Remigio Nicoli could not have known that Díaz would launch a successful sorbet business. All he knew was that his wife had to use her property as collateral. In marriages such as these, where wives ostensibly had property and the husband did not, the credit risk was compromised not only by the husband's lack of funds but also by his lack of a reputation in the market.

The interest rates that married women paid were interest rates on their husbands. Relying on a wife's personal assets was a public indicator of economic duress or inexperience, and it signaled to creditors, past and present, that the husband who allowed his wife to use her property as collateral on a loan either did not have any property of his own or was willing to pay a higher interest rate to keep his own property safe. The interest-rate premium charged to married women was a measured response to the *implication* of their borrowing, namely, that husband and household were less creditworthy and that loans to married women were much more closely associated to the real risk presented by their husbands than to any risk embodied in the women themselves.

Chapter Six

Monopoly, Continuity, and Change
The Case of José Anacleto Patrón Zavalegui

The requirements of the notarial public record were increased,
but so were the incentives toward monopoly.
—Notarial Law of Yucatán, 1915

The role of notaries, from the Spanish colony to the independent republic's banking system, highlights the capitalist transformation of Yucatán. Notaries became financial intermediaries of this transformation, as Yucatán's private mortgage market—effectively the precursor to the formal credit market that banks would eventually become—developed in their offices.[1] This last chapter focuses on the personal networks of one notary and his role in capital mobilization and credit allocation.

In a pattern that resembles the concentration of power in other industries in Mexico, the growth of Yucatán's mortgage market relied heavily on the growing support and power of one single actor. In Yucatán, this actor was a notary, one solitary operator in an increasingly active market that relied ever more on his services and expertise. José Anacleto Patrón Zavalegui's story reveals his transformation from notarial apprentice to Yucatán's leading notary. His growth into a monopolist notary is a fitting example of the intricate pattern of entrepreneurship and concentration that has so often been repeated in Mexico and throughout Latin America.

Patrón Zavalegui and Credit Markets

Much like their French counterparts during the eighteenth and nineteenth centuries, notaries provided the intermediation that connected private borrowers to long-term credit during Yucatán's henequen boom. Mérida, however, unlike Paris, was small, geographically removed from the national capital, and ethnically heterogeneous. While Mexican and French notaries shared very similar legal texts and codes, the context in which they exercised them determined the many differences between them. Unlike France, Mexico was still a relatively young postcolonial republic, where Mexican wealth was centralized and concentrated. Political favoritism permeated Mexican society, fostered entrepreneurial innovation, and cemented social inequalities. In short, the henequen boom was both a boon to entrepreneurial tradespersons and the urban economy, but it did so without improving the conditions for women or indigenous Mayas or the majority of the population.

The transformation of Yucatán's credit market suggests ways in which innovation and entrepreneurship coexisted with traditional forms of exchange and privilege. The contracts notaries wrote and the personal relations they established with their clients were part of a tradition harking back to the early fifteenth century in colonial Mexico and Spain, and in the same vein, the success of one of these notaries in creating a near monopoly over the mortgage market in the late nineteenth century should be considered as an innovation in a traditional industry. However, this notary's success and subsequent control of the market mirrored trends among Mexican entrepreneurs who created monopolies and conglomerates. The close connection between capital investors and governments, especially in Mexico, favored the interests of investors at the expense of consumers, and it privileged early success in any industry, thereby making it very difficult for latecomers to participate or succeed.

The Patrón Zavalegui story is the microhistory of this pattern. As the only notary who also had a seat in the state Congress, he had an early exposure to the political networks of the city and went on to garner control over the recording of more than 75 percent of the city's contracts and mortgages, exercising influence among the parties to these contracts and keeping potential competing notaries at bay. The role of intermediary developed for Patrón Zavalegui in the context of the boom and his ability as a notary to respond to the two-pronged demands of the agricultural export market. On the one hand, the market needed secure long-term credit for agricultural production; on the other hand, it needed a reliable information flow to support the contractual agreements that would provide these long-term credits. Patrón Zavalegui's success was the product of three overlapping conditions: first, he lived in Yucatán at the time of boom; second, he became a notary when banks didn't lend long-term and after usury restraints had been lifted; and third, his social network put him closer to the inner circle of politics in Yucatán than any other notary.

José Anacleto Patrón Zavalegui was born in 1839, the son of a notary who had also been mayor in the early independence period. Through his mother he was connected to early Spanish nobility of colonial Yucatán—his great-great-great-grandfather on his mother's side was also mayor in the early 1700s. By the nineteenth century, Patrón Zavalegui's family had joined the ranks of the liberal professions and was part of what we could call Mérida's middling elite. But by any measure, Patrón Zavalegui's success as a notary was exceptional. From 1875 onward (when he started recording contracts) to the end of the century in 1899 (close to when this study's data set ends), Patrón Zavalegui was at the center of a process that changed not only the nature of the economy but also the nature of his profession. Over the next three decades, the notaries of Yucatán would oversee a growth in the provision of mortgage credit in line with the growth in the henequen market, but incomparable to anything expected from notaries until then. By the end of the century, Patrón Zavalegui had become the most popular notary in town, recording more than three-quarters of all contracts, including mortgage contracts.

Patrón Zavalegui received an education similar to that of lawyers, as a result of the 1865 law that reinforced the legal training of notaries.[2] Mexico City notarial students presented their qualifications and application to Mexico's only notarial school, the Colegio de Escribanos, but Patrón Zavalegui became a notary by presenting his completed exams and degrees to the Yucatán Ministry of Justice and the superior tribunal courts in the capital, Mérida.[3] This last step gave him the title of notario, but a particular notarial office and the notarial seal had to be allocated by the local civil court (in Mérida) that assigned offices as they became available.[4] As in the European notarial tradition, each notarial office in Mérida was assigned to one specific notary, who then sold or transferred his office to another notary. Patrón Zavalegui's office, Notaría 5, was not transferred until after his death and the Mexican Revolution in the early twentieth century.

The notarial profit structure was very different from that of banks. In their role as facilitators of mortgages, notaries did not take deposits, issue notes, charge interest rates, or issue any loans. As a result, notaries took on none of the financial risks that banks assumed. A notary's income came exclusively from the fees charged per document, fees that were regulated and established by the local Congress. Unlike banks or traditional brokers, notaries did not earn commissions on their transactions, and their income was exclusively a reflection of the volume of their transactions. Not only did notaries mediate the financial structure of the boom without profiting directly from it, but they also took on a reputational risk by engaging in this intermediation. They risked their reputation by informally vouching for the creditworthiness of the borrowers they tied to lenders in the contracts they recorded.

If Patrón Zavalegui's ledgers are any indication, his bulging, leather-bound volumes attest to the extension of his network and the reach of his reputation toward the end of the century. Where most notaries filled at most one ledger per year, Patrón Zavalegui filled four per year at least. These ledgers constitute one of the most important aspects of Patrón Zavalegui's role in the economy, because they contain so much information about his clients. The personal relationships that are inherent in credit transactions developed over time, and Patrón Zavalegui's success in this business was tied to the size of his client list and the longevity of his clients. The information chain that he recorded in his ledgers as well as the personal relationships he developed with his clients during their lifetime put him in a position to vouch informally for the reputation of anyone who transacted regularly through his office, and in this way Patrón Zavalegui, more than any other notary, moved beyond the role of record keeper into that of information broker.

Nowhere is the importance of José Anacleto Patrón Zavalegui's role in the credit market more apparent than when we consider that he recorded not only more private mortgage loans in the late nineteenth century than any other notary but also more mortgages than any bank, even after banks had opened (see fig. 6.1). In 1895 notaries recorded nearly nine hundred thousand pesos in mortgage loans in Mérida, almost twice as much as the total outstanding loans of the two Yucatecan banks that opened five years

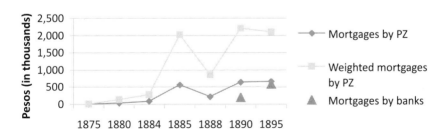

Fig. 6.1 Comparison of Patrón Zavalegui's portfolio and local bank mortgages
SOURCE: Protocolos notariales, AGEY and ANEY; "Balance promedio de bancos."

earlier, and Patrón Zavalegui was responsible for more than 75 percent of that amount.

The mortgage market that developed in Patrón Zavalegui's office and the short-term credit market provided by banks grew proportionately during the henequen boom. Fig. 6.2 shows that Patrón Zavalegui's record of long-term mortgages is comparable to the banks' total portfolio of liabilities and provides another piece of the evidence that connects the informal credit markets to the rise of regional banking in Mexico.[5] These bank liabilities included short-term trade credit, reserve funds, banknotes issued, and outstanding credit accounts. This figure, as well as fig. 6.1, demonstrates that banks were a supplementary source of credit in Yucatán, but that they could not satisfy the local demand for credit. Patrón Zavalegui's ledgers contain documentary evidence that banks could not even lend to their own board members; in 1890 and 1895 Patrón Zavalegui recorded mortgages between members of both banks' board of directors.

While banks supplied credit and liquidity to the economy, mortgages remained the only source of long-term lending and borrowing for planters and investors, and Patrón Zavalegui's office provided access to long-term credit. It was the absence of banks and the absence of long-term credit from banks that secured the position of notaries such as Patrón Zavalegui as the main conduits to long-term credit in Yucatán.

Market Share and Scope

Nothing in Patrón Zavalegui's early career suggested he would become such an important notary. Like all other notaries in Mérida, Patrón Zavalegui had an office that was centrally located within a short walk of the

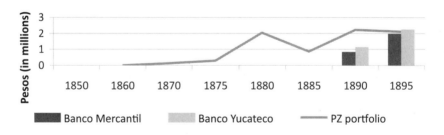

Fig. 6.2 Comparison of Patrón Zavalegui's weighted portfolio with two local banks' total liabilities (short and long term)
SOURCE: Protocolos notariales, AGEY and ANEY; "Balance promedio de bancos."

central plaza, the seat of local government, and all his other colleagues in the profession.[6] Patrón Zavalegui's address, 519 Calle 67, placed him farthest from the plaza and the seat of government along the western edge of the main square of Mérida, but all notaries as per the 1896 city directory lived or worked within four blocks of the Gran Plaza in the center of town.

Patrón's success cannot be linked to any obvious social prominence; he was not a member of any wealthy henequen family, and both his marriages were unions of modest social relevance. He had one child in his first marriage to Angela Cisneros, who had no discernible connections to Yucatán's elite families, and the marriage ended when she died in the mid-1860s. He was soon remarried to Petrona Evia, a seamstress from a small town north of Mérida and the adopted child of one of his fellow Congress members and lay priest, Francisco Evia.[7] While his client list and congressional career suggest he attained professional and political prominence, there is no evidence of him having become a notable member, let alone a leader among the intellectual or financial elite. His ambition seems to have been restricted to his profession, from which he profited more than other notaries only because he worked more than his peers. He recorded the largest share of mortgage contracts, and through these he developed lucrative contacts with the main henequen producers and traders. Apart from his short tenure in the State Congress and a posthumous note about his death, Patrón Zavalegui's name never appeared anywhere else, except in his ledgers.[8]

What we do know, however, is that as the number of mortgages he recorded increased, so did the number of other contracts he recorded. Most striking are his number of sales contracts. As fig. 6.3 illustrates, Patrón Zavalegui recorded an ever-greater share of sales contracts after 1875, the year he started recording contracts, and the trend suggests he would soon be recording a comparable share of sales contracts.

The columns show the number of sales contracts in the sample and the proportional increase in the number of sales contracts Patrón Zavalegui recorded. His contracts started only in 1875, when he wrote his first contracts while he was still an apprentice of two well-established Mérida notaries, Manuel Ávila Maldonado and Eligio Guzmán. His training served him well, perhaps better than his mentors ever expected. Soon after he acquired his own office, his recording activity gradually eclipsed that of his mentors and all other notaries.

Even if borrowers usually followed their lender to their chosen notary to record a mortgage, the key relationship in this market was not between lenders and borrowers but between the notary and his clients. Among the

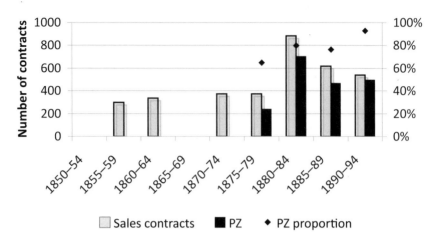

Fig. 6.3 Patrón Zavalegui's share of sales contracts
SOURCE: Protocolos notariales, AGEY and ANEY.

clients, those that stood to gain the most from their relationship with a notary were potential borrowers. Bibiano Aguilar, for example, borrowed in 1890 and 1895 only through the offices of Patrón Zavalegui, even when Aguilar was mortgaging property outside of Mérida. Borrowers in general rarely borrowed more than once in a year (except in 1885, when an increased proportion of them borrowed a higher number of times), and when they did, they never borrowed from the same lender twice. If there was any measure of constancy in their borrowing pattern, it was that, like Bibiano Aguilar, they signed all those mortgages in the same office with the same notary.

Borrowers tended to return to the same notary for successive loans, and in every year except 1860, loyal borrowers accounted for at least 50 percent of the mortgages. Because borrowers did not determine the choice of notary (this was a decision left to the lender), this loyalty suggests that the notary connected loyal borrowers to the lenders he knew. This loyalty and its underlying logic reveals that, as Patrón Zavalegui's share of the mortgage market grew, he would have also orchestrated interactions between lenders and borrowers about whom he had increasing amounts of information. Although this group of repeat borrowers was small, the relationship with Patrón Zavalegui was an important one, especially as repeat borrowers started borrowing more and started an almost exclusive relationship with Patrón Zavalegui after 1885.

This exclusivity, of course, had a reason: in an economic climate of high expectations about economic growth, the information Patrón Zavalegui had from the recording of contracts and documents revealing his clients' wealth and reputation became important assets of his office. The possible benefits of this information fostered the interest of potential borrowers in Patrón Zavalegui, who was known to have a large and generous client network. Table 4.7 in chapter 4 shows Patrón Zavalegui's rising market among his colleagues. Patrón Zavalegui's ability to crowd out his competition relied largely on his ability to attract new borrowers and new lenders in Mérida's mortgage market. This ability was firmly anchored in the early part of his career. He developed his early reputation between 1875 and 1885, and in the aftermath of an important loan for the construction of a railroad in 1885, the rest of his career relied on his ability to attract a steady stream of new clients while retaining the old ones. This ability is illustrated in fig. 6.4, where Patrón Zavalegui's clients are tracked from the first time they signed a credit contract in his office. The lines illustrate Patrón Zavalegui's rate of new client capture, which was calculated by tagging each client in each year from 1875 onward and identifying them in the data set in the successive years.[9]

The graph makes the convincing case that Patrón Zavalegui courted new clients most actively between 1875 and 1883, the years before the railroad financing deal. Because he was just starting his career, all of his clients were new in those years, as he struggled to compete with the already well-established notaries. By 1884 a small proportion of them were returning clients who knew Patrón Zavalegui from previous years, and the line of new clients continues to fall as his developing and successful relationships with his clients were rewarded with clients who interacted with him in

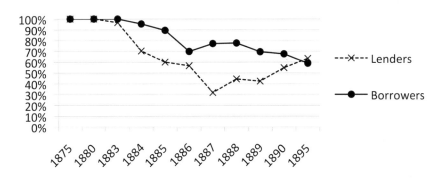

Fig. 6.4 New clients for Patrón Zavalegui (proportion of new to old)
SOURCE: Protocolos notariales, AGEY and ANEY.

more mortgage transactions. The falling line is a good thing—it indicates increasing stability in a gradually maturing client base.

Fig. 6.4 shows Patrón Zavalegui developing an increasingly loyal client base as his position at the heart of the notarial mortgage market solidified, and he built on his success in the early 1880s. In these years he attracted returning clients to his office and laid the foundations of the relationships that eventually led to the railroad deal. The graph reveals one of the keys to Patrón Zavalegui's success: between 1875 and 1886 he developed his office in Mérida and acquired professional recognition and a solid reputation. When new lenders and borrowers entered the mortgage market in response to the henequen boom, Patrón Zavalegui's ability to attract them and maintain a stable rate of returning clients reinforced his position among the Mérida notaries.

Fig. 6.5 further illustrates the underpinnings of Patrón Zavalegui's client base. Patrón Zavalegui was successful at attracting not only the most clients to his office but also the big clients who lent and borrowed large amounts. This graph illustrates the contributions of lenders (old and new) to an increasingly new set of borrowers. The difference between figs. 6.4 and 6.5 is a crucial one in explaining Patrón Zavalegui's role in this market.

Fig. 6.5 shows how new lenders funded the pool of novice borrowers—a positive consequence of the stability demonstrated in graph 6.4. Loans to new borrowers outweighed loans by new lenders after 1885, as new and old capital was mobilized during the boom. As the mortgage market grew, Patrón Zavalegui's client list expanded and started to include lenders and borrowers who were not directly involved in the henequen economy, even if the mortgage market funded mostly agricultural producers and traders, and Patrón Zavalegui's intermediation in the market reinforced the link

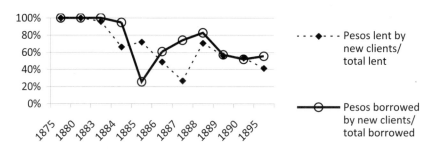

Fig. 6.5 Proportion of amounts lent and borrowed by new clients of Patrón Zavalegui

SOURCE: Protocolos notariales, AGEY and ANEY.

between henequen and entry into this market as a borrower. While borrowers, especially those who were loyal to Patrón Zavalegui, tended to be closely tied to the henequen business, the notary's stable client list could lend beyond it, which is precisely the sort of diversification that is good for economic development. The institutional arrangement that Patrón Zavalegui and his peers offered in the early years of the boom evolved to serve additional and new borrowers—providing an institution capable of financing nonhenequen and non–export-oriented borrowers.

The Railroad Deal

Not only did José Anacleto Patrón Zavalegui become one of the most prolific notaries of Mérida during the last quarter of the nineteenth century, he was also the only notary who was a member of the state Congress at the time of this study. Like any other notary, Patrón Zavalegui recorded land deeds, commercial associations, wills and testaments, and guardianships of minor children, but he also found time to develop another career in public service. He became a substitute member of the local Congress in 1886, and in 1890 he was elected as senior member of the Yucatán Congress. His political career overlaps not coincidentally with the largest structured mortgage loan recorded in Yucatán, which Patrón Zavalegui recorded in his office in 1885; his career took a radical and upward turn after recording this loan—a loan that brought together the new Yucatecan fortunes and the developing regional railroads.

In 1885, ten years after training to become a notary, Patrón Zavalegui recorded three separate mortgage contracts to raise funds for the fledgling railroad companies in Yucatán. The three mortgage contracts raised a total of Mex$214,765 in 1885 and were unique not only because they raised so much money but also because they coordinated a large number of lenders, most (but not all) of which were involved in the production or trade of henequen.[10] From 1885 on, no other notary would rise as quickly or dominate the city's clientele as strongly as José Anacleto Patrón Zavalegui.

The Financiers

Toward the turn of the century, Yucatecan investors would finance their infrastructure projects by selling equity and pooling investors in shareholding companies, but in 1885 the financing of large-scale infrastructure projects remained a personal affair. The Yucatán government had granted railroad developers concessions earlier in the year to build railroads in response to the foreign demand for henequen. Developers would, in turn, be responsible for raising the money to clear the land, bring in the materials and the machinery, build the line, and run freight along it, without any financial support or backing from the local or national government.

Railroads developed in Mérida in response to the boom, and they eased and hastened the transport of henequen between plantations and the port from which henequen bales were shipped out to American ports. Unlike other Latin American railroads, the Yucatecan ventures were largely financed, owned, and operated by domestic partners.[11] Francisco Cantón was one of these early investors in railroads who began building a trunk line between Mérida and his hometown of Valladolid in the 1880s. Francisco Cantón had been a general in the local army, a veteran of the internecine rural and indigenous civil war known as the Caste War in the late 1840s, and would later be President Porfirio Díaz's personal choice for governor of Yucatán between 1898 and 1902.[12] General Pancho Cantón, as he was known, won the lucrative concession early in 1885 on the basis of his wartime reputation and the expectation that he would be able to secure financing to build it, which he did through the first and largest of the railroad loans Patrón Zavalegui recorded.

Cantón never participated in the henequen business directly but became involved in its development by being at the heart of the transportation network that sprung up around it. In 1885 he borrowed Mex$170,000 from thirty different lenders to build a railroad from Mérida to Valladolid. This first loan and all successive ones were recorded at the offices of Patrón Zavalegui. Following the 1885 loan, Pancho Cantón borrowed at least three more times from different lenders, using his trunk line concession as collateral in mortgage contracts issued through Patrón Zavalegui's office. General Cantón's case was something of an exception in a market where borrowers typically followed lenders to their notary. In this case, however, the borrower was so famous and the economic climate so heated that lenders probably flocked to the deal.

Why the general chose to do this deal through Patrón Zavalegui is open to conjecture. Patrón Zavalegui became a member of congress in 1886, and perhaps the two had met in private political meetings, or the general chose Patrón Zavalegui because he had known his brother, Carlos Roberto, a member of the conservative forces during Mexico's national Reform War in the 1850s. Carlos Roberto Patrón Zavalegui fought in support of the conservative forces and against republican rule in the 1850s, and in late 1860 Carlos Roberto became the interim governor of the recently invaded city and state of Aguascalientes. When liberal forces overthrew the conservative government there, he was caught and executed. This sacrifice of a local son had garnered him respect among the Yucatecan elite, and it is not impossible that, as a fellow soldier and fellow conservative during those wars, General Cantón would have remembered the episode twenty-five years later when he turned to the surviving Patrón Zavalegui brother, José Anacleto, to help him structure a securitized loan contract.

A different set of Cantóns, Olegario and Rodulfo (who were only distantly related to General Cantón), received another concession to build a railroad, this one from Mérida to the southeastern town of Peto.[13] They, too, secured a mortgage in 1885 through the office of Patrón Zavalegui. The borrowers had borrowed small sums previously in 1880, and for this purpose they followed their lenders, as was customary, to their notary (who wasn't Patrón Zavalegui). The brothers started working with Patrón Zavalegui in 1884, when they made very small loans to other Mérida residents through his office. After the 1885 loan they obtained through his office, the brothers borrowed repeatedly through lenders that worked exclusively with Patrón Zavalegui.

In 1885 General Cantón and the Cantón brothers raised almost Mex$220,000, by mortgaging the land they had purchased to build the railways. The largest of the contracts was the general's. He borrowed Mex$170,000 from thirty different investors for a six-year period at a cost of 12 percent interest per year. Previously he had mortgaged successive pieces of the land along the line to finance the initial construction; all of these smaller mortgage deals had also been handled through Patrón Zavalegui's office. In July 1885 Olegario and Rodulfo Cantón had raised funds by mortgaging land adjacent to the land on which they were building their railroad. Their contract, too, was recorded in Patrón Zavalegui's office.[14] At Mex$15,000, the Cantón brothers' mortgage was significantly smaller and also significantly cheaper, because they paid only 6 percent per year for a six-year mortgage. The railroad line on which they took out the mortgage was finally completed in 1889, while Francisco Cantón's line did not reach its farthest destination in the city of Valladolid until 1907, with significant additional help from investors and the government (his tenure as governor of the state between 1898 and 1902 probably helped).

Many investors in the 1885 railroad mortgages recorded by Patrón Zavalegui were henequen planters with haciendas close to the railroad lines who would remain on Patrón Zavalegui's client list for decades. The rise of Patrón Zavalegui also cemented his relationship with the lenders and borrowers in these deals. Just as all the Cantóns remained loyal to Patrón Zavalegui, so did the investors in the deal, who returned to his office in subsequent years. The effect of this loyalty by the railroad investors is illustrated in fig. 6.6. The graph shows the weight of lenders from the railroad deals in Patrón Zavalegui's office. The dotted line represents the peso amount of loans these lenders made through José Anacleto Patrón Zavalegui (referred to in the legend as "PZ"), and the solid upper measures all mortgage loans they made, including those they recorded in Patrón Zavalegui's office.

The 1885 contracts caused a ripple in the Mérida market, because unlike most mundane transactions that a notary handled, these contracts were talked about and generated a certain excitement. Their size and their relevance to the local infrastructure created publicity about railroad development, which in turn had a corollary effect on young Patrón Zavalegui's career. It provided publicity for his office and his ability to structure a complicated contract, and it reinforced his trustworthiness in handling matters of long-term finance with a cadre of illustrious clients.

Consequently, not only did the railroad investors continue to work with Patrón Zavalegui, but also new potential lenders were more likely to approach him. Before 1885 investors in the railroad deal quite understandably interacted more with notaries other than with Patrón Zavalegui, because Patrón Zavalegui was just developing his office in those years. But from 1885 on, more lenders and borrowers recorded their mortgages with him than with any other notary and would continue to do so year after

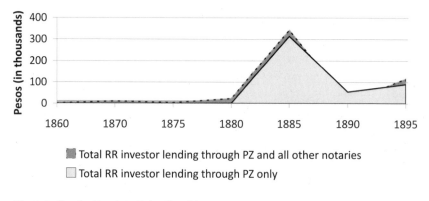

Fig. 6.6 Patrón Zavalegui's lending history
SOURCE: Protocolos notariales, AGEY and ANEY.

year. After the railroad deals in 1885, Patrón Zavalegui went on to become the most important notary in the city.

Life After the Railroad Deal

After Patrón Zavalegui opened his own office, he was no longer like any other notary in Mérida. After structuring the railroad deal in 1885, he successfully poached clients from his old mentor and competitor Ávila Maldonado. Other clients moved to his office after having previously dealt with José Andrade, another competitor. For example, Manuel Zapata Bolio lent Mex$10,000 to Miguel Peón through the office of José Andrade in 1885. In 1890 he lent a minor sum of Mex$600 to Josefa Espinosa de Navarrete, this time through Patrón Zavalegui. In 1895 Zapata Bolio's lending profile exploded as he made nine loans for a total of Mex$137,000. All were handled through Patrón Zavalegui's office, and they amounted to almost one-fifth of Patrón Zavalegui's mortgages that year.

Manuel Dondé Preciat was another lender who worked exclusively through Patrón Zavalegui's office after being one of the investors in Pancho Cantón's deal in 1885. He contributed Mex$16,077 to the Mex$170,000 loan, but before his involvement in that deal, he had made only one loan in 1875 through notary Ávila Maldonado, and in 1880 another one through notary Francisco Flota. But between 1885 and 1895, all except one of his mortgage loans went through the office of Patrón Zavalegui.

Table 6.1 highlights Patrón Zavalegui's recruitment of clients from 1875 through 1895. The table charts the exodus from his greatest competitor, Ávila Maldonado, and focuses on the movement of clients who recorded loan transactions at least twice between 1870 and 1895.[15] Clients who chose Patrón Zavalegui as their notary for their first mortgage loan (as depicted in the fourth column) tended to stay with him for future loan contracts (column 6).

Patrón Zavalegui's talent lay not only in keeping existing clients but also seemingly in seducing clients away from other notaries. As table 6.1 indicates, until 1885, twelve of the nineteen first-time clients transacted with Ávila Maldonado. This preference is explained by Ávila Maldonado's experience and longevity in Mérida, which most likely contributed to his reputation among the citizens of Mérida. However, five of these initial clients of Ávila Maldonado's eventually moved to Patrón Zavalegui's office and in future contracts transacted exclusively with Patrón Zavalegui, as the last column indicates. As of 1885 (and as of the railroad mortgages),

Table 6.1 José Anacleto Patrón Zavalegui (PZ) versus Manuel Ávila Maldonado (MAM)

Year of first mortgage	Total number of mortgages	Name of client	First notary	First mortgage with PZ	Exclusively with PZ or definite switch to PZ
1870	7	Felipe Vado	MAM	1885	Yes
1875	2	Simón Cáceres	PZ	1875	Yes
1875	2	Gertrudis Vado	PZ	1875	Yes
—	9	José María Celarain	MAM	1884	No
1875	16	Manuel Dondé Preciat	MAM	1884	No
1875	30	O'Horan Hospital (institution)	MAM	1885	No
1875	12	Victoriano Nieves	MAM	1885	No
1875	4	Prudencio Hijuelos	MAM	never	No
1880	3	José Rafael de Regil	PZ	1880	Yes
1880	15	Cosme Ángel Villajuana	PZ	1880	Yes
1880	5	Gregorio Cantón	MAM	1884	Yes
1880	8	Joaquín Quijano	MAM	never	No
1882	5	Marcos Duarte Ruela	MAM	1885	Yes
1882	60	Eduardo Peón	MAM	never	No
1882	6	Carlos Peón	MAM	1885	No
1883	2	Santiago Peniche	MAM	1890	Yes
1884	10	Nicolás Almeida	PZ	1884	Yes
1884	6	Dolores de la Guerra de Mendoza	PZ	1884	No
1884	3	Augusto Peón	PZ	1895	Yes
1885	11	Francisco Martínez Arredondo	PZ	1885	Yes
1885	2	Pedro Palma	PZ	1885	Yes
1885	2	Pedro Peón Contreras	PZ	1885	Yes
1885	14	Manuel Zapata Bolio	PZ	1885	Yes
1888	2	Camila Ramírez	MAM	1895	Yes
1888	4	Juan Urcelay	PZ	1887	Yes
1890	3	Eusebio Escalante Bates	PZ	1890	Yes
1890	2	Adolfina Rendón Quijano	MAM	1895	Yes

SOURCE: Protocolos notariales, AGEY and ANEY.

new clients tended to choose Patrón Zavalegui as their notary and transacted mortgage contracts solely through him.

This trend most likely has much to do with the market's perception of Patrón Zavalegui's position within it, and the behavior of borrowers in this market proves how important he was in the specifics of this dynamic. It also contributed to Patrón Zavalegui's enormous share of mortgages. Concentration of power has long been a constant in Mexican history, and it was clearly a trend in Yucatán, where Patrón Zavalegui's market share grew in concert with Olegario Molina's share of the henequen trade, but this sort of concentration of notarial power was highly atypical in the profession.[16]

Undoubtedly, part of the explanation of Patrón Zavalegui's appeal to his new clients was his overwhelming success and the fact that he was the first notary to garner such publicly demonstrated trust from some of Yucatán's elite. Trust in personal connections was an important currency in this market, especially in political networks. Patrón Zavalegui benefited not only from his insertion in the local social network from his notarial training but also by his connection to political circles. His reputation would have conferred trust. Another aspect that probably made him attractive to clients and built on his trustworthiness was his connection to the city's big lenders, which greatly increased his business. The 1885 deal put Patrón Zavalegui in the public eye, as it connected him to a very specific, rare, and highly desirable asset in a booming economy—access to long-term credit.

Chapter Seven

Conclusion

For the better part of human history, banks were not the most important financial intermediaries, and in many parts of the world today, banks are far from being the only one.[1] Although capital markets and banks have become essentially synonymous in many places, banks are not accessible to many potential users; instead, lenders and borrowers may interact through non-bank intermediaries such as rotating savings associations or microfinance companies, or in extremis, loan sharks and pawnshops. Many of the lessons from Yucatán's nineteenth-century mortgage market described in the previous chapters transcend geography and time and are relevant in the twenty-first century. The question of how an economy responded to chronic shortfalls in credit and lapses in the provision of credit not only is an interesting historical problem but also reflects problems that are being addressed in current-day Latin America and certain parts of the United States as well.[2] The success of organizations such as Acción Internacional in Latin America, Grameen Bank in India, or Compartamos in Mexico, as well as many other microfinance companies, has less to do with their ability to counter endemic poverty through the provision of small and renewable loans and more to do with the inability of traditional banks to reach beyond their limited network of depositors and borrowers. The goals of notaries in the nineteenth century and microfinance companies today are radically different, but their role in financial history originate in a similar place, namely the dearth of credit.

Notaries at the Center

This book has analyzed notaries as intermediaries and the circumstances under which mortgages became crucial to the functioning of the credit market in Yucatán. Notaries became unwitting financial intermediaries during the henequen boom; they were not trained to develop mortgage networks among their clients, but their access to information about the parties with whom they interacted supported their function at the center of the local credit market. Notaries also became intermediaries because certain events and circumstances created opportunities for them. The lifting of usury bans, the end of the Caste War, and the henequen boom all contributed to the growth of private financial markets, and in the absence of banks, supported the role of notaries in these debt markets. Benito Juárez's liberalization of interest rates in 1861 was a legal change that had a profound effect on the credit market of Yucatán: it allowed the price of credit to be explicit and legal for the first time. As the boom expanded the Yucatecan economy, labor relations were equally redrawn and refocused. Capital was devoted to henequen, labor was drawn onto plantations, and land was mortgaged to raise more capital. The financing of Yucatán's boom relied on informal and formal mechanisms that permeated society, tying workers to hacienda owners, henequen traders to henequen producers, and investors to borrowers. And at the center of this intricate web sat the notaries.

The analysis of the mortgage market that arose during the henequen boom in Yucatán demonstrates that a lack of formal credit brought forth informal credit and that notaries provided the necessary trust and guarantees through their informal network. Although trust was and still is the main currency of all financial transactions, it was an essential component of intermediation, especially before modern banks internalized this trust. In most of the world and for the better part of history, a very broad set of individuals, institutions, and occupations have performed the role of embodying trust and managing the information that supports it; notaries are a very good example of this type of prebank financial intermediary in the Americas.[3] Notaries drew on their main asset: information to foster and generate trust. The staples of a notary's daily business—wills, guardianships, land sales, and mortgages—provided notaries with significant amounts of information about their clients and their potential client base. Such information, especially the sales contracts, was central to their relationship with lenders and borrowers.

The role of notaries in Mérida's credit market had more to do with their informal function than the formal definition of their profession. The repeated interactions they had with their clients through the recording of many different types of contracts was the glue that connected them to a network of lenders and borrowers. More important, it was their position in the middle of that network that rendered them so important in the credit market—a position that garnered information and built trust, two essential components of credit relations. Lenders trusted that notaries would protect their interests and safeguard their information, and borrowers trusted that notaries could provide connections to lenders; thus, the flow of information created a credit market before banks.

Property Rights and the Mortgage Market

Intangible elements such as trust can hold people and contracts together, but also grasping the subtle rules of the game, for example social norms and legal practice, is key to understanding the economic incentives and constraints that dominated the Yucatán mortgage market. As this book has shown, the lifting of usury laws had an observable and immediate impact on the Yucatán mortgage market, but other laws had equally important effects on the scale and the scope of the mortgage market. The distribution of credit and the variation in the cost of credit demonstrates that property rights, as defined in the Mexican civil codes, could constitute significant obstacles to the allocation of credit. The imbalance in property rights between men and women in Mexico is crucial in understanding how credit markets worked, as well as *who* could participate in them. Law and economics overlapped in Yucatán, as the civil laws protected the integrity of the family estate and also weakened women's property rights, establishing a dynamic in which women could own but not use property, and husbands had no rights over the property they were, by law, entrusted to manage— leading to a division between use and management of property. This scission increased both the real and perceived risk of a married woman, who, when she did borrow, did so not for her own purpose, but for the purpose and use of her husband, who sat with her at the notary's office, consenting to a transaction that existed solely for his purpose. The existence of this male partner, who had no rights *to* her property but had most rights *over* her, damaged the seamlessness by which ownership should have granted access to credit. Thus, the reason mortgages to married women carried higher interest rates was rooted in the public sphere's perception of them as creditors, where the existence of a husband signaled to lenders specific risk factors (above and beyond those related to the legal constraints associated with gender) that affected their interest rate. We would not be able to understand this aspect of the credit markets if we did not understand the legal framework that underpinned these markets.

Notarial Monopoly

The laws, institutions, and trust that formed the notarial role in credit markets were not immune to the monopolizing tendency in Mexico's nineteenth-century markets. José Anacleto Patrón Zavalegui's entrepreneurial success reflected both the entrepreneurial context of Yucatán's boom and the underlying parameters of success in nineteenth-century Mexico, and it wouldn't be until the Mexican Revolution that these parameters would be questioned. When the revolutionary army of General Alvarado declared a new notarial law in 1915, the stated purpose was to undo the "incentives toward monopoly" in the profession.[4] Had Patrón Zavalegui not died in July 1907, Alvarado might very well have been speaking about him.

Not only did José Anacleto Patrón Zavalegui command almost the entire mortgage market by the end of the nineteenth century, he did so without having any financial stake in it, save for a stake in his own reputation. As the local economy grew, and notaries connected private borrowers to long-term credit, Patrón Zavalegui helped those lenders and borrowers who gained access to his network, which undoubtedly resulted in positive financial rewards for him (although such rewards cannot be substantiated in the historical record). Except for his office ledgers and a few mentions in the congressional record, we know very little about the notary who would, at the end of the century, have information about almost every lender and borrower in Mérida.

His rise and preeminence among notaries was a response to the two-pronged demands of the henequen market, which needed (1) secure long-term credit and (2) a reliable information flow to support the contractual agreements that would provide such long-term credit. Patrón Zavalegui demonstrated he could deliver the first (he structured an important railroad deal), and he satisfied the second over the course of successive interactions with an ever-widening client network. In a context of less-than-perfect information flows, Patrón Zavalegui acquired the trust of the market first, and in so doing, he also gained the largest share of this market.

Like the trading-house magnates and henequen barons, José Anacleto Patrón Zavalegui profited from being in Yucatán when the boom started, from being a notary when banks did not lend long-term, and from being closer to the inner circle of politics in Yucatán than any other notary. His success emphasizes the importance of personal connections in the development of credit markets, even more so in incipient markets where information is scarce and formal institutions are missing. In Yucatán's bankless economic boom, Patrón Zavalegui was the harbinger of the capitalist transformation of Yucatán. His colleagues contributed to the transition, as did the henequen traders and producers and the entire productive system that arose in Yucatán, and together they all exemplify the central role of personal networks and connections during economic transitions.

Notaries Survive Henequen's Demise

The henequen boom would start to slow by the turn of the century. By 1903 the price of henequen dropped significantly, and the popular press of the time, as well as many scholars since, blamed the fall on the perceived collusion between henequen traders and the International Harvester Company (who had become the main purchaser of henequen in the late nineteenth century).[5] It is much more likely that the fall in the price of henequen was a response to the increasing productivity of plantations and the greater supply of henequen, further signs of the capitalist transition of the region.[6] The turn of the century also saw Yucatán facing competition from other fiber and twine producers, followed by the Mexican Revolution. The outcome of the revolution reorganized the henequen business without immediately challenging the henequen traders, but by the end of World War I, the looming threat of plastics spelled the definitive end of Yucatán's henequen era and made a significant dent in the local credit market. Henequen crumbled as the bedrock of the Yucatán economy, but the notaries are, to this day, still there.

Appendix

Regression Analysis from Chapter 5

Table A.1   Regression analysis of women's interest rate variables

Interest rate (constant)	9.52
Marital status	coef: −2.23
(married/unmarried, including	SE: 1.06
widows)	t-stat: 2.10
Length of loan (short term/long	coef: −.47
term)	SE: 1.21
	t-stat: −.40
Location of collateral	coef: 2.26
(urban/rural)	SE: 1.28
	t-stat: 1.72

Source: Protocolos notariales, AGEY and ANEY.

Gender had a significant effect on the price paid for credit in all the years sampled and among all the borrowers. The regression was estimated over the entire period, with dummy variables for marital status (0 if married, 1 if not married, including widows); length of loan (0 if less than one year, 1 if one year or more); location of collateral (0 if urban, 1 if rural); and size of loan (0 if less than one thousand pesos, 1 if one thousand pesos or more). The t-stat measures statistical significance, and the results are significant (i.e., not due to a random numerical error) when the t-stat is above 2 (SE stands for standard error). The constant is the constant term of interest rate in the regression equation. The coefficient calculates the effect on the interest rate for a change in value of the variables. In the regression, marital status was identified as 0 if the female borrower was married, and 1 if widowed or unmarried. The negative sign on the coefficient signifies that for a value of 1 in the variable, the interest rate will be 2.23 times higher than if the variable were 0. Similarly, if the loan was large, the interest rate would be 2.26 times smaller. The t-stat measures the statistical significance.

The data from the notaries' records establishes a number of explanatory variables that could cause the interest-rate hike: marital status and gender, professions, place and date of birth, detailed descriptions of collateral (including geographic location), and the size and term of the loan itself. Using these variables as markers for the regressions, the results show that marriage more than any other variable affected women's interest rates. The same regression using male borrowers yielded a low coefficient of no statistical significance, suggesting that the marriage penalty affected married women only.

What Was a Peso Worth?

Aurora Gómez-Galvarriato and Aldo Musacchio's price indices are the best to attempt a time-value adjustment of nineteenth-century prices.[1] Unfortunately, the data starts in 1886 and the adjustment percentages are based on textile industry prices. The Veracruz textile industry had no overlap with the Yucatán henequen industry, and the two local markets were quite different, separate, and distant. However, it is the best indicator available, and I have used this index when calculating real loan amounts in fig. A.1.

I also used the simple currency exchange to make adjustments, especially when addressing henequen prices that were quoted on the interna-

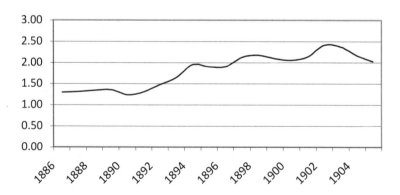

Fig. A.1   Mexican peso to U.S. dollar exchange rate
SOURCE: Estadísticas económicas.

tional market and consumed by the U.S. market. In this context, the best measure of a peso was its value in dollars.

It would not be wise to adjust local prices and local interest rates using the U.S. currency exchange rate. The relationship between the U.S. dollar and the Mexican peso was stable until the last fifteen years of the century, so an index using currencies would not reveal much. The Galvarriato-Musacchio index is still better.

That said, one of the best and most illustrative ways to understand what the amounts discussed in the book may have represented and what they meant to those borrowing or lending can be found in the contracts used in this book. The price and value ascribed to consumer goods and real estate in probate inventories and sales contracts paint an anecdotal picture that is difficult to aggregate into a reliable index.

The case of José Calero Cano, who died in 1874, is a case in point. He was a thirty-six-year-old pharmacist when he died and left a widow, Ana Rivas y Domínguez, and five children under the age of ten. Manuel Ávila Maldonado was the notary who handled the inventory, and he hired specialists to value the assets: José León Castillo for the home itself; Francisco Gómez Pérez for the library; master silversmith Enrique Basulto for the jewelry; pharmacist Joaquín Dondé for the inventory of the pharmacy; and carpenter Juan López for the decorative art and other furniture in the home. The inventory included a long list of personal items, as well as an exhaustive list of his pharmacy's inventory, with amounts and prices for each individual item. Table A.2 is a translated summary of the original inventory, which is twenty-five pages long.

Table A.2 Inventory of the Calero Cano estate

	Value (pesos)
Inventory of Pharmacy (La Catedral)	
Cash	
In cash box	229.75
Held by Celestino Ruiz del Hoyo, employee	1500.00
Jewelry	
A dozen silver spoons (twenty-seven ounces, one peso/ounce)	27.00
Bust of the Dolorosa	8.00
Pharmaceuticals	
Medicinals (twelve pages of inventory)	6,591.70
Homeopathics	394.31
Library (books on pharmacy shelves)	
Twenty books about physics, medicinals, pharmacopeia	79.00
Measuring tools	457.43

(continues)

Table A.2 *(continued)*

	Value (pesos)
Furniture	402.40
Inventory of Home	
Furniture	
Twenty-seven cane chairs in good condition	42.50
Five cane chairs in poor condition	7.50
Four rocking chairs	24.00
Two small sewing chairs	7.00
One mirror with mahogany frame	20.00
One wardrobe	2.00
One varnished cedar table	5.50
One cedar bassinette	8.00
One tin bathing tub (very used)	1.50
One board and 1 domino set	2.00
One microscope	6.00
Library (on bookshelves)	
One Bible in Vulgate Latin, nineteen *tomes* [volumes?]	10.00
Philosophical Studies on Christianity (by A. Nicholas)	5.00
Catechism of Perseverance (by Gaume) incomplete	4.00
French-Spanish dictionary	3.00
Don Quixote de la Mancha	5.00
Ensayo histórico de las revoluciones de Yucatán	1.50
Farm animals	
Two goats	18.00
One fattened pig *(cerdo cebado)*	42.00
Real estate	
One house in Mérida	1,250.00
(The house had nine arches around a central patio, five bedrooms, a living room, a kitchen, a laundry room, a coal room, a larder, a horse barn, four patios, a well, and iron railings along the outside windows.)	
Debts	
To his wife	1,800.00
To his sisters Juana, Antonia, Pilar, and Concepcion Calero	500.00
Total assets (including pharmacy)	**12,645.70**
Total liabilities	**2,300.00**
The inventory also accounted for expenses made during the drawing up of the inventory such as:	
Food for the family, July 12–31, 1874	70.00
One casket	66.00

SOURCE: Box 192–13, Sucesiones Testamentarias, Fondo Ejecutivo, AGEY.

NOTE: An existing copy of Serapio Baqueiro's *Ensayo historico de las revoluciones de Yucatán* was published in 1878, four years after the death of Calero Cano and this inventory. The Miami University of Ohio owns a microfilm copy of a previous edition from 1873. Calero Cano probably owned one of these early copies.

This inventory of a middle-class pharmacist of respectable wealth reveals more than his preference for nonfiction literature or the contents of his well-appointed apothecary. It is also an inventory of the cost of the goods that any Yucatecan citizen incurred. It is an inventory of a world where a mirror was worth more than a chair, and a casket could cost as much as food for a family of six for three weeks. In other words, it is the inventory of a world not unlike ours.

Notes

Chapter 1

1. Levine, "Financial Development." In "Universal Banking," Caroline Fohlin also identifies three types of services that banks and intermediaries provide: brokerage (matching investors and borrowers), qualitative asset transformation (altering the liquidity or maturity of financial claims), and portfolios (diversifying assets, especially those too expensive for a single investor).

2. See, for example, Greif, "Contract Enforceability"; Ensminger, *Making a Market*; Burns, *Colonial Habits*; Gay, *Moneylenders*; Finn, *Character of Credit*; Frank, *Dutra's World*; and Olegario, *Culture of Credit*.

3. Specifically for Mexico, see Marichal, "Obstacles to Development," and more generally for the entire colonial period, see Robinson and Acemoglu, *Economic Origins*.

4. There had been an earlier Banco do Brazil founded by King João when the Portuguese royal family exiled itself to its colonies during the Napoleonic Wars, but this bank was more of a royal treasury, and it failed when João returned to Portugal in 1821, taking the bank assets with him.

5. The commercial code outlining specific bank charter regulations in 1884 and enforcing state supervision over these charters was crucial in the expansion of banks in Mexico; see Maurer, *Power and the Money*.

6. Greif, "Contract Enforceability; Finn, *Character of Credit*; Wiemers, "Agriculture and Credit."

7. Remmers, *Henequen*; Wells, "All in the Family"; Joseph and Wells, *Summer of Discontent*.

8. The importance of the distinction between market norms and social norms has been explored by Dan Ariely in *Predictably Irrational*. In chapter 4, Ariely discusses an experiment that neatly outlines the difference between the world of social norms (where behavior is modeled according to reputation and socially constructed parameters) or market norms (which are structured around material incentives).

9. On informal relations in markets, see Bell, Srinivasan, and Udry, "Interlinking Credit Markets"; Besley and Levenson, "Role of Informal Finance"; Levenson and Maloney, "Informal Sector"; MacMillan and Woodruff, "Interfirm Relationships"; Roberts, "Informal Economy"; and Sudhanshu and Claremont, "Economics of Rotating Savings." A very small sample of the scholarship studying informal mechanisms of credit distribution includes Hoffman, Postel-Vinay, and Rosenthal, *Priceless Markets*; Bottin, Jeannin, and Pelus, *Marchands d'Europe*; Francesca, "Merchants and Money"; Lemercier, *Un si discret pouvoir*; Lemercier, "L'institution et le groupe"; Guinnane, "Cooperatives"; Granovetter, "Strength of Weak Ties"; Franklin and McKinnon, *Relative Values*; and Botticini, "Tale of 'Benevolent' Governments."

10. In *First Men of Cajamarca*, James Lockhart pioneered work using native language documents, primarily notarial contracts, and so began a long scholarly tradition of using

their documentation. Robert Patch, in *Maya and Spaniard*, and Terry Rugeley, in *Maya Wars, Wonders and Wise Men*, and *Yucatán's Maya Peasantry*, have taken different and very successful approaches with similar native- and Spanish-language sources in Yucatán, as have other scholars of Latin America, especially Bert Jude Barickman, in *Bahian Counterpoint*, and Muriel Nazzari, in *Disappearance of the Dowry*, for Brazil. European scholars have also relied on the records of notaries for similar purposes.

11. Haber, *Industry and Underdevelopment*, 21.

12. For example, pawnshops, one of the oldest operating short-term credit providers, did not stop during the independence wars or the revolution; see François, *Culture of Everyday Credit*.

13. Marichal, *Las inversiones extranjeras*; François, *Culture of Everyday Credit*.

14. See Wiemers, "Agriculture and Credit," and Haber, *Industry and Underdevelopment*.

15. See Hoffman, Postel-Vinay, and Rosenthal, *Priceless Markets*.

16. Triner, *Banking and Economic Development*; Musacchio, *Experiments in Financial Democracy*; Ludlow and Marichal, *Banca y poder*; Haber, "Industrial Concentration," "Financial Markets"; Del Ángel-Mobarak, *Paradoxes of Financial Development*; Maurer, *Power and the Money*.

17. Haber, "Industrial Concentration."

18. Marichal, *Las inversiones extranjeras*; Marichal, "Obstacles to Development."

19. Cerutti and Marichal, *La banca regional*.

20. Hanley, *Native Capital*; Sweigart, "Brazilian Export Agriculture"; Ridings, *Business Interest Groups*.

21. Von Wobeser, *El crédito eclesiástico*; Brading, *Miners and Merchants*; Florescano and Gil Sánchez, *Época del las reformas*.

22. Van Young, *Hacienda and Market*; Greenow, *Credit and Socioeconomic Change*.

23. Tenenbaum, *Politics of Penury*; Chowning, *Wealth and Power*; Van Young, *Mexican Regions*.

24. Wasserman, *Capitalists, Caciques, and Revolution*; Walker, *Kinship, Business, and Politics*; Saragoza, *Monterrey Elite*.

25. For recent analysis of the role of kinship and insider networks and the effects of the colonial legacy on economic development, see Haber, *Industry and Underdevelopment*; Maurer, *Power and the Money*; Haber, *Crony Capitalism*; Haber, Razo, and Maurer, *Politics of Property Rights*; Robinson and Acemoglu, "Economic Backwardness"; and Robinson and Acemoglu, *Economic Origins*.

26. Granovetter, "Strength of Weak Ties." Also see Lynne Zucker's approach to trust in nonkin transactions in "Production of Trust."

27. North, *Economic Performance*; De Soto, *Other Path*. The connection between Porfirian privatizations and unrest in the countryside has long been recognized among historians of the Mexican Revolution. For some of the most famous analyses, see Knight, *Mexican Revolution*; Katz, *Pancho Villa*; and Womack, *Zapata*.

28. For Yucatecan historical studies on the use of notarial records in Yucatán for the early and midcolonial period, see Farriss, *Maya Society*; Quezada, *Pueblos y caciques yucatecos*; and Restall, *Maya World*.

29. Hoffman, Postel-Vinay, and Rosenthal, *Priceless Markets*; Hardwick, *Practice of Patriarchy*; Merwick, *Death of a Notary*.

30. Van Bochove, "Intermediaries"; Burns, *Colonial Habits*; LeGrand and Corso, "Los archivos notariales."

31. Hanson-Jones, *Wealth of a Nation*, 5.

32. Frank, *Dutra's World*.

33. Some of the books that have addressed the financial activity of widows within the broader scope of their arguments are Greenow, *Credit and Socioeconomic Change*; Nazzari,

Disappearance of the Dowry; Arrom, *Women of Mexico City*; Twinam, *Public Lives, Private Secrets*; Gauderman, *Women's Lives*; and Korth and Flusche, "Dowry and Inheritance."

Chapter 2

The epigraph to this chapter is drawn from Mason, "Green Gold of Yucatán."

1. In Paris, the ratio of private mortgage loans to population in 1840 was five in a thousand; see Hoffman, Postel-Vinay, and Rosenthal, *Priceless Markets*, 255, 274.

2. David Brading's seminal study of mining in Mexico, "Miners and Merchants," explores the Bourbon reorganization of the silver mining industry, which transformed Mexico into the world's leading silver producer and financed the revival of the Spanish monarchy in the late eighteenth century.

3. Patch, *Maya and Spaniard*.

4. See Moreno Fraginals's "*El ingenio*" for a classical approach to the sugar industry in Cuba, and Dye's *Cuban Sugar* for a more contemporary view.

5. See "Principales productos." In *Maya and Spaniard*, Robert Patch has argued that traveling merchants actually connected the Yucatán peasants and haciendas to the mining towns farther north, but it would be difficult to characterize Yucatán in the colonial period as anything more than a small and local economy.

6. Rodríguez Losa, *Geografía política de Yucatán*.

7. The later census of the Mérida population performed by Serapio Baqueiro in 1881 is more widely accepted and puts Mérida's population in 1881 at 42,925 people; see "Reseña geográfica."

8. For figures and accounts of foreign migration to Yucatán in the nineteenth century, see Suárez Molina, *Evolución económica*; Ota Mishima, *Destino México*; and Bojórquez Urzaiz, *Emigración cubana*.

9. Joseph, *Rediscovering the Past*.

10. John Taylor, *Maximilian and Carlotta*, 113.

11. Haber, "Political Economy."

12. Remmers, *Henequen*.

13. Castro, *Informe*.

14. Evans, *Bound in Twine*, 35.

15. Echánove Trujillo, *Enciclopedia yucatanense*.

16. The Solís machine was named after its inventor Leopoldo Solís; see Echánove Trujillo, *Enciclopedia yucatanense*.

17. Suárez Molina, *Evolución económica*.

18. *Estadísticas económicas del Porfiriato*.

19. Reed, *Caste War of Yucatán*.

20. Wells, "All in the Family."

21. "Testamentaria de Dn. José Calero Cano, vecino que fue de Mérida," Ramo Sucesiones Testamentarias, 192–13, Fondo Poder Ejecutivo, AGEY.

22. Sánchez Novelo, *Recreación en Yucatán*.

23. In *Leisure Class*, Thorstein Veblen most eloquently addressed the issue, which in turn was placed in a Yucatecan context by equally eloquent historians of the region; see Wells, *Yucatán's Gilded Age*; Joseph and Wells, *Summer of Discontent*; Joseph, *Revolution from Without*; and Rugeley, *Yucatán's Maya Peasantry*.

24. Lutz, Prieto, and Sanderson, *Population, Development, and Environment*.

25. For more specific analyses of the church and ecclesiastical power in Yucatán, Mexico, and the Americas, see Kathryn Burns, who paints a fascinating picture of the role of the church and ecclesiastical norms in colonial Latin America in *Colonial Habits*. William

B. Taylor describes the centrality of the church in the formation of the colonial Mexican society in *Magistrates of the Sacred*, and for Richard E. Boyer's analysis of the ways in which Mexicans sidestepped ecclesiastical expectations, making it all the more obvious how important the church was in colonial society, see *Lives of the Bigamists*. More specifically for Yucatán, Nancy Farriss, in *Maya Society*, and Robert Patch, in *Maya and Spaniard*, use the diocese archives to draw a picture of Yucatecan society and economy as it was recorded in the ecclesiastical record.

26. Karen Caplan's *Indigenous Citizens*, an excellent analysis of the politics of liberalism in Yucatán, offers insight into the complexities of the relationship between indigenous institutions and state governments.

27. See specifically González Navarro, *Raza y tierra*; for a more tempered approach, see Rugeley, *Yuactán's Maya Peasantry*.

28. Rugeley, *Yucatán's Maya Peasantry*.

29. Ibid.; Rugeley, *Maya Wars*; Rugeley, *Wonders and Wise Men*.

30. Jacinto Canek led an indigenous rebellion in the eighteenth century, which was neither particularly widespread nor violent, but it sent the nonindigenous Yucatecans into a panic over the lack of control they perceived themselves as having over the Maya. The Caste War and the contemporary and historical response to it reemphasize this distance and distrust between indigenous and nonindigenous in Yucatán.

31. Reed, *Caste War of Yucatán*.

32. Remmers, *Henequen*; Lapointe, *Mayas rebeldes*; Abreu-Gómez, *Conjura de Xincum*; Dumond, *Machete and the Cross*.

33. Dumond and Streichen Dumond, *Demography and Parish Affairs*.

34. In *Indigenous Citizens*, Karen Caplan uses the same approach to identify ethnicity.

Chapter 3

The epigraph to this chapter is quoted from the 1870 printed text of the Código de la Reforma, first enacted in 1861.

1. Mexican bank charters were attractive because they conferred exclusive note-issuance rights, a highly attractive asset in cash-strapped economies. The Commercial Code of 1884 banned all banks without federal charters from issuing notes.

2. For example, see Noonan, *Scholastic Analysis of Usury*; Nelson, *Idea of Usury*; and Tan, "Usury Prohibition."

3. Of course, these regulated rates were relevant in official markets only, and there is enough evidence of usurious lending by loan sharks and the ubiquitous *agiotistas* (speculators and usurers) of the nineteenth century.

4. *Leyes de la Reforma*. Contemporary newspapers and commentators made no apparent issue of the decree, but legal scholars referred to it. The issue provoked some interest almost a century later in the Mexican legal journal *Jurídica*, which devoted a special issue to usury. See Borja Martínez, "Usura."

5. The 1861 decree reads, "Que en uso de la facultades de que me hallo investido, he tenido a bien decretar lo siguiente: Art 1. Quedan abrogadas en toda la República las leyes prohibitivas del mútuo usurario; Art 2. En consecuencia la tasa o interés queda a voluntad de las partes"; see *Leyes de la Reforma*.

6. Cunningham, *Foreign Policies*.

7. The first emperor was Agustín de Iturbide, a general in the war of independence, who was proclaimed emperor of Mexico in September 1822 and fled the throne in 1824. His was the first of many governments following the end of Spanish rule in Mexico. See

Kinsbrunner, *Independence in Spanish America*. For a different approach to this period in Mexico's history, see Van Young, *Other Rebellion*.

8. The colonization plans of the French imperial armies were geared at increasing the number of new Mexican citizens who would recognize them as legitimate and encourage investment and innovation in Mexico; see Dabbs, *French Army in Mexico*, 238–40.

9. As a lender, the church was especially powerful in the Bajío, as Linda Greenow, in *Credit and Socioeconomic Change*, and Eric Van Young, in *Hacienda and Market*, have demonstrated.

10. The literature on this aspect of the Bourbon reforms is rich, especially because the Consolidación de Vales Reales and many of the other revenue-generating reforms in the Spanish colonies in many ways provoked the discontent that would spark the independence revolution in 1810. Spain "gained revenue and lost an Empire," as Lynch states in *Bourbon Spain* (21). See also Hamnett, "Appropriation"; Lavrin, "Execution of the Law"; Greenow, *Credit and Socioeconomic Change*, 26; and Chowning, "Consolidación de vales reales."

11. The church's support of usury controls in canon law was fraught with contradictions, because the church had to accommodate the doctrine to commercial circumstances that were themselves beneficial to church finances; see Le Goff, *Money or Your Life*.

12. Borja Martínez, "Usura."

13. The mid-nineteenth century saw the repeal of usury laws in Great Britain and in most of the United States. The earliest usury repeal was in Alabama in 1818, and in 1881 North Dakota was the last to repeal usury laws. The state of Nevada repealed usury laws in 1861, the same year Mexico did. See Rockoff, "Prodigals and Projectors."

14. See Coatsworth's now classic article, "Obstacles to Economic Growth." See also Coatsworth, *Growth Against Development*; Haber, *Industry and Underdevelopment*; Cardenas, "Macroeconomic Interpretation"; Marichal, "Obstacles to Development"; and Maurer, *Power and the Money*.

15. Many historians consider this such a truth that they don't even address the assumption. Thomas Luckett puts it nicely in the context of European usury bans: "There probably never was a time in European history when usury laws actually prevented lenders from charging interest" ("Credit and Commercial Society," 31).

16. Bernabé Vargas to Laureana López, mortgage contract, March 23, 1860, for Mex$108, repaid on August 4, 1860. Notario Ladislao Cantón, libro 203, AGEY.

17. Tan, "Empty Shell"; Rockoff, "Prodigals and Projectors"; Temin and Voth, "Financial Repression."

18. In "Financial Repression," Peter Temin and Hans Joachim Voth prove a similar point.

19. See Evans, *Bound in Twine*.

20. I limit the discussion to debt instruments available to private entities and leave aside public finance and government debt.

21. See von Wobeser, *El crédito eclesiástico*; and Greenow, *Credit and Socioeconomic Change*. In my data, in 1850 ecclesiastic loans represented 12 percent of the total funds lent through notarial offices, and in 1860 the church was responsible for no more than 3 percent of the total funds lent through the notarial offices. In data from 1870 and later, the church is entirely absent.

22. Ludlow and Marichal, *Banca y poder*; Haber, "Financial Markets"; Maurer, *Power and the Money*.

23. Bank notes were not a common form of exchange, and silver and metal coins were the base currency. A shortage of metal coins created complications for exchange, payment of salaries, and supplies. The creation of banks that could issue and back notes significantly eased those restrictions.

24. Joseph and Wells, *Summer of Discontent*.

25. In *Barbarous Mexico*, John Kenneth Turner writes most incriminatingly about debt-peonage as "de facto" slavery, a perspective that has been repeated in more recent literature. See also Joseph, *Revolution from Without*.

26. In *Yucatán's Gilded Age*, Allen Wells gives an account of servant (im)mobility and loss of independence as a result of indebtedness. For a more recent study, see Alston, Mattiace, and Nonnenmacher, in "Coercion, Culture, and Contracts."

27. The importance of the relationship is a point made mostly by anthropologists. Clifford Geertz's seminal work, *Peddlers and Princes*, perhaps best describes these social contexts of commercial relationships. A more geographically applicable approach to the social context of debt in Mexico is explored in the French volume edited by Chamoux and others, *Prêter et emprunter*.

28. Piedad Peniche Rivero goes so far as to suggest that the purpose of the hacienda was labor reproduction, not productivity. She sees the haciendas as a locus of complex relations that disempowered workers by integrating them into an artificial collaboration within the hacienda hierarchy. In "Comunidad doméstica," she demonstrates the mobility of the female employees on a hacienda in Umán, Yucatán, between 1860 and 1869. Granted, this period was not the height of the boom, but it suggests loopholes in the residential aspects of peonage.

29. Box 161-D, Fondo Justicia, AGEY.

30. Walton, *Civil Law in Spain*.

31. The average size of Maya estates was less than two thousand pesos in this period; see table 2.5 for details.

32. Box 161-D, Fondo Justicia, AGEY.

33. Box 183-CH, Fondo Justicia, AGEY.

34. Box 161-D, Fondo Justicia, AGEY.

35. The discussion in chapter 2 on the inequality of wealth between indigenous and nonindigenous illustrates the chasm in wealth distribution, as well as the significantly lower rate of growth in wealth among indigenous people.

Chapter 4

The epigraph to this chapter, drawn from *Novísimo escribano instruido*, reads as follows: "La buena fama es la reputación que un hombre goza entre sus semejantes de ser justo y estricto cumplidos sus deberes; sin ella la autoridad que la ley concede al escribano carece de su más preciosa y sólida base." The Mexican proverb is "más vale buena fama que cama dorada."

1. Diego de Godoy is said to have undersigned the foundation of the settlement of Villa Rica de la Vera Cruz in 1519; see *Memorias del III Congreso*.

2. Pérez Fernández del Castillo, *Apuntes para la historia*.

3. This description of the educational prerequisites is taken from Pérez Fernández del Castillo's *Historia de la escribanía*, which reproduces many of the codes, *reglamentos*, and decrees pertaining to the notarial function in Mexico.

4. Yucatán notaries could also choose to become affiliated with the *Academia del Colegio de Escribanos*, which was the Mexican notary association in Mexico City. At the time it was incorporated with the *Colegio de Escribanos* (the national notarial college); where the Mexico City notaries got their degrees. See Pérez Fernández del Castillo, *Historia de la escribanía*.

5. A copy of the December 12, 1908, official gazette of the Mexican government, the *Diario Oficial*, records a new Notarial Law of Yucatán, which includes a rare list of the ranges for the fees notaries could charge to record documents in their ledgers. Nothing

suggests that these fees were not made public or widely known in the nineteenth century. See "Arancel de notarios", art. III, cap. 12, *Ley del Notariado.*

6. This fee schedule stems from the following case, initiated by a notary against one of his clients who did not pay the fees or costs of a sales contract in Mérida, June 25, 1884. *Juicio verbal seguido por el notario José A. Patrón Zavalegui contra Ignacio Vado González por deuda de pesos por la alcabala de una escritura de venta que otorgó en su favor don José M Alcocer* (Legal suit of the notary José A. Patrón Zavalegui against Ignacio Vado Gonzalez for debt of pesos owed on taxes of a sales deed by don José M. Alcocer). Box 146, Fondo Justicia, AGEY (1).

7. The civil code required the registration of any contract that affected or might affect the ownership status of a piece of property. *Código Civil del Estado,* arts. 1979, 1980.

8. In 1850 usury constraints still ruled the world of credit, and in Yucatán approximately 16 percent of loans were not explicitly backed by collateral. This proportion gradually fell as the market expanded and interest rates rose. By 1880 only 2 percent of loans recorded by notaries were noncollateralized.

9. These noncollateralized or nonnotarized loans would have relied on other enforcement mechanisms such as reputation, but such informal contracts are outside the scope of this study, unless, of course, they were notarized.

10. These liberal reforms began with the Ley Lerdo in 1856, were formalized in the 1857 constitution and further emboldened by Benito Juarez's presidential victory in 1861, and were aimed at breaking down the stranglehold of the church on Mexican land ownership and bringing progress to the Mexican economy. The process of privatization and commercialization continued throughout the nineteenth century. Under Porfirio Diaz (1876–1910) the land reforms supported the privatization of village lands and are part of the explanation of the land concentration in Yucatán and elsewhere in the country, which was one of the driving causes of the Mexican Revolution between 1910 and 1917.

11. There were more notaries in Mérida than appear in table 4.2, but they did not appear as signatories on any credit contracts in the years analyzed. This sampling technique does not leave out any potential significant notaries that I might have missed had I not sampled and analyzed every year between 1850 and 1895. Large-scale and important notaries recorded loans regularly, and a summary review of the ledgers that were not included in the sample confirms that participation was fairly constant.

12. This is a conservative average, because I considered the end of my observation period as the end of the life of all notaries, which significantly biases the life span of those notaries who entered the scene late in the period.

13. Although the *Registro de notarios* registered all notaries when they began their careers, these records have not survived. These figures, therefore, represent the notaries that signed contracts in the ledgers in each year of analysis between 1850 and 1895.

14. The figures in the last column of table 4.3 can be replicated by adding the two largest market shares in each year from table 4.2.

15. See Ensminger, *Making a Market.*

16. Unlike Manuel Gómez Morín, who after the Mexican Revolution, overtly acted as a financial and political adviser and lobbyist on behalf of his clients, notaries interacted with their clients in a much more ad hoc way; see Recio, "Abogado y la empresa."

17. Lamoreaux, *Industrial New England.*

18. Remmers, *Henequen;* Wells, "All in the Family"; Joseph and Wells, *Summer of Discontent;* Carrillo, *Secretos de familia;* Pérez Sarmiento, *El cultivo.*

19. The probate records show some evidence of private intrafamily loans that were to be repaid by the estate, but these did not represent the proportion of loans one might have expected if kinship lending was the prevalent form of finance.

20. The sample of contracts includes every mortgage contract a year at five-year intervals between 1870 and 1895 and a ten-year interval between 1850 and 1860.

21. The measure of kinship I use is based on the Latin American tradition of recording the maternal and paternal surname for men and unmarried women and of recording the husband's surname in the case of married women. In the later part of my analysis starting around 1880, the contracts also recorded the name of the borrower's spouse, even if the spouse was not a party to the contract.

22. Ledgers of José Anacleto Patrón Zavalegui, 1890, Fondo Notarial, AGEY.

23. The 1895 census report accounts for adult population by birth origin and reveals the migration effect on population levels.

24. I borrow the term "loyal" from Hoffman, Postel-Vinay, and Rosenthal's *Priceless Markets*.

25. I cannot say if this loyalty extends to other contracts that do not carry the inherent default risk of credit contracts (such as wills or guardianships).

26. Ecclesiastical finance was nowhere near as important in Yucatán as it had been in other parts of Mexico, but institutional lending was one of the rare forms of formal lending before the boom. The liberal reforms that confiscated church property were reflected in this way in the mortgage records.

27. The variability of the results in column 4 of table 4.6 is an effect of the bias injected in the measure of repetition, since repetition is counted only within a given year.

28. In the eighteenth century, Paris credit market notaries provided similar services as the Mexican notaries did in Yucatán. However, while Parisian notaries segmented the market by contract specialty, their market shares were nowhere near as disparate as those seen among the Mérida notaries. See Hoffman, Postel-Vinay, and Rosenthal, *Priceless Markets*.

29. Menéndez, *90 años de historia*.

30. The details of the 1890 loan are as follows: September 9, 1890, Mex$4,000 at 12 percent per year for four years, with a yearly repayment of Mex$1,333 in henequen starting in year two. The collateral was a *paraje* (plot) in Conkal, and the lender, Eusebio Escalante Bates, was the owner of a large trading house in Mérida. The contract included an obligation by the borrower to sell all the henequen grown on the collateralized plot to Escalante Bates at the quoted price at Escalante's trading house. If the borrower sold his henequen to anyone else, the contract would terminate and repayment of principal would be immediate. In 1895 Ricardo Zapata loaned Mex$1,500 to Bibiano Aguilar on January 3, 1895 at 6 percent per year for five years, collateralized with a house of 4,608 square varas in Conkal; Juan Sáenz loaned Mex$699 to Bibiano Aguilar on March 12, 1895, at 12 percent for two years, collateralized with a plot of land in Conkal, which was also already mortgaged for Mex$200 to Emilio Cásares.

31. These figures, however, do not mean that borrowers rarely accessed the mortgage market again; they just did not do so in any of the years sampled.

32. There were also lawyers and doctors who owned land or were members of families who grew and traded henequen. They usually stated both occupations in the contracts.

33. These occupations are some of those stated among the borrowers who appeared only once.

Chapter 5

The epigraph to this chapter is drawn from ledger 360, Protocolos del notario José Andrade, 1891, AGEY. It reads, "En Mérida de Yucatán, a los diez días del mes de Febrero de mil ochocientos noventa y un años. Ante mí, José Andrade, notario público del Estado y testigos que se expresarán, comparecieron el Señor Don Lorenzo Peón de cuarenta y siete años de edad, proprietario, casado con la Señora Doña Cleta Cásares, ejercitada en faenas de su sexo, de cuarenta y siete años de edad, quien concurre prestando su consentimiento para la validez de éste instrumento, ambos vecinos de ésta ciudad, según expresaron y a quien doy fe conocer, el primero Señor Peón dijo: que la Señora Doña Candelaria Escalante Duarte le ha tenido concederle a mútuo la suma de cuareta y cinco mil pesos que de ella ha recibido y que le pagará de ésta forma: cinco mil pesos el diez de Febrero de mil ochocientos noventa y dos, cinco mil pesos el diez de Febrero de mil ochocientos noventa y tres, diez mil pesos el diez de Febrero de mil ochocientos noventa y cuatro, diez mil pesos el diez de Febrero de mil ochocientos noventa y cinco, diez mil pesos el diez de Febrero de mil ochocientos noventa y seis, y cinco mil pesos el diez de Febrero de mil ochocientos noventa y siete, y desde la fecha el interés de seis porciento anual que entregará por mensualidades vencidas. . . ."

1. Property rights are a central mechanism of economic interaction. For a review of seminal works in this literature and economic history analyses that use some of the key concepts of the New Institutional Economics, see North, *Economic Performance*, 129–57; and Engermann and Sokoloff, "History Lessons."

2. For more work on the legal and economic role of women in Latin America during the late nineteenth and twentieth century, see especially the work of Deere and León, *Empowering Women*; Deere and León, "Married Women's Property Rights"; and Hamilton, "Property Rights."

3. This statement excludes indigenous Maya women, because the mortgage market is almost entirely devoid of Maya parties.

4. Anglo-Saxon coverture laws merged a wife's legal rights with those of her husband, and unlike the Spanish colonial codes, provided few exceptions before the nineteenth century.

5. Like indigenous Mexicans, all women, children, and the poor were considered to be weaker members of society, requiring special protection. In the case of women, legislative restrictions on their freedom were presented as a means to protect them from being unduly influenced by unscrupulous people (presumably men); see Arrom, *Women of Mexico City*, 71–81. The nineteenth-century reforms to private laws began a series of reforms concerning the poor and the indigenous, but the legislative position toward women scarcely changed before the Mexican Revolution and the 1917 constitution; see Mirow, *Latin American Law*.

6. The Maya residents of Yucatán were the region's largest and most marginalized ethnic group, yet they owned property, as seen in public records of land sales, land deeds, and probate inventories. Nevertheless, in the notarial ledgers debtors or creditors with Maya surnames are quite rare.

7. In "Dowry and Inheritance," Korth and Flusche provide a concise overview of the Castilian legislation that provided the framework for much of the Latin American laws, including those concerning women.

8. Arrom, *Women of Mexico City*, 84. Examples of women's legal exclusion are found in the American or British legal systems, which reserved even fewer rights for women until the nineteenth century.

9. I say "relative independence" because, while widows and unmarried women had similar property rights to those of men (barring age limits), in practice they continued to be female and maintained their status as weaker members of society, with the requisite consequence on their property rights. Thus, widows were able to manage their own property, but not that of their minor children and the coheirs of their husband's estate.

10. Arrom, "Mexican Family Law."

11. In 1895 Mex$30,000 was roughly equivalent to US$15,625; see appendix.

12. There are only three cases in which women lent to women, and the scarcity of these cases suggest that women as lenders did not choose or give preferential treatment to female borrowers.

13. The most common biases associated with probate inventories is that the sample may not be representative of the entire population, because it often ignores the poor and includes a disproportionate number of elderly among the dead, who have a disproportionate level of wealth compared to the younger and the living. There are also many sampling difficulties in probate analyses. Here probates were sampled randomly among the boxes in the Poder Ejecutivo section of the Archivo General del Estado de Yucatán. Other archive sections also contain probates, but it is a stroke of luck to find them. The sample of 379 probates between 1847 and 1901 includes more than 100 Maya probates, and many probates with small to valueless inventories.

14. Unlike the examples recorded by Carmen Diana Deere and Magdalena León in "Married Women's Property Rights," testamentary freedom in Yucatán did not lead to wives being favored in husband's wills.

15. The debts from 1895 and 1901 were owed Candelaria by her daughter, her niece, and at least twenty other businesspersons and tradespersons in Mérida. The debts took the form of straightforward mortgage loans, collateralized by land, as well as short-term commercial loans, which Candelaria overwhelmingly issued to tradespersons and henequen planters. Sección Testamentos: Inventario de los bienes de la difunta Candelaria Castillo de Villajuana, January 30, 1901, Poder Civil, AGEY.

16. These summary findings are the result of calculations based on 379 probate inventories from Mérida for the period of 1850–1905. The probates were sampled randomly throughout the period, as the boxes in which they are stored in the archive became available. Seventy of the probates belong to women, both Maya and not, who died in Mérida or one of the surrounding parishes. The main reasons why an estate went into probate were complicated estate divisions (these were the cases involving large fortunes) and the survival of minor children, which biases the sample in favor of wealthy women and poor mothers of minor children. In these cases, the probate proceedings were a way to prove the poverty and indigence of the parent and the need for the courts to enforce the choice of a guardian.

17. José Anacleto Patrón Zavalegui, libro 392, Notaria Publica 5, ANEY.

18. José Anacleto Patrón Zavalegui, libros 303 and 393, ANEY.

19. *Boletín estadístico.*

20. Having claimed their half of the marital property at the death of their husbands (as was guaranteed by the laws governing community property), widows (and widowers) were comparatively wealthier than their married or never married counterparts. This is not unlike the ending practices among women in the colonial period, as Greenow shows in *Credit and Socioeconomic Change.*

21. The focus has rarely been on property rights per se in the colonial literature, but the legal context looms large as the structure within which the role of gender and the lives of women are analyzed; see Arrom, *Women of Mexico City*; Socolow, *Colonial Latin America*; Seed, *Love, Honor and Obey*; and Twinam, *Public Lives, Private Secrets.*

22. Table 5.2 starts in 1880 because the ecclesiastical ban on usury created an artificial cap on interest rates until the early 1870s. The usury ban was supported in civil law and made it illegal to charge more than 6 percent on private loans and 5 percent on commercial loans. Any record of interest rates until then is rather inconclusive, especially because the constraints caused by the usury ban led to widespread underreporting of interest rates in the mortgage contracts.

23. The effect of gender on interest rates in the data set yields a coefficient of 1.53, with a t-stat of 2.91. See appendix for regression analysis.

24. These rationales for risk evaluation did not preclude the possibility of interest-rate manipulation, which ecclesiastical edicts on usury were designed to control, but these were no longer in effect by the late 1870s. Even in such cases, usuriously high interest rates were

still a reflection of the *perceived* risk of the borrower, even if this was the perception of a prejudiced or rapacious lender. In any case, usury bans were lifted in 1861 when Benito Juarez decreed the abolition of the civil laws that supported them in debt contracts. His decrees were not overturned during the Second Empire under Maximilian, and by 1870, all mortgage contracts recorded by the Mérida notaries had interest rates well above the pre-1861 maximum of 6 percent.

25. Tutelage is the legal term used in the documents to refer to the protection or guardianship conferred onto the weaker member of society who is put *bajo tutela*—literally "under protection." It was enforced and reinforced in the civil codes of Yucatán, for example, in the following articles in the 1870 Civil Code. Article 205: The husband is the legitimate administrator of marital assets, and article 206: The husband is the legitimate representative of his wife; see *Código Civil del Estado*.

26. Silvia Arrom, in *Women of Mexico City* and "Mexican Family Law," suggests that by the middle of the nineteenth century, dowries were no longer a main component of a bride's wealth, and her point is confirmed in the official record of Yucatán, where not one single dowry contract appears in the notarial ledger names. This does not mean that women no longer owned assets before they got married, but it suggests that family property and the traditional mechanisms of transmission of wealth within the family structure were changing. It is beyond the scope of this book to speculate about or analyze this phenomenon. See also Nazzari, *Disappearance of the Dowry*.

27. More research on Yucatán inheritance patterns will allow for greater understanding of the conditions and circumstances under which the *mejora* and the *quinta* were used, which respectively gave parents the right to favor one child with up to one-third of the restricted estate or with one-fifth of the unrestricted estate. The mejora was abandoned in the 1870 Civil Code of the republic. In *Wealth and Power*, Margaret Chowning shows that the distributive principle was so strong that before 1884, testators in Michoacán rarely availed themselves of the opportunity under the law to reserve one-fifth of the estate for someone other than the wife or children or to bequeath to a favorite child. Even after 1884, testators continued to divide their estate equally among their children.

28. There are enough cases of husbands (and wives) accusing their spouse of adultery in the civil court files of the AGEY to suggest that these constraints were not enough to curb certain passions. Nevertheless, it was extremely rare for wealthy members of society to accuse their spouse of infidelity. The laws further improved the chances that by maintaining a wife under tutelage and control, a husband's legitimate fatherhood would not be easily doubted by either the father or his social circle. For a recent study, see Twinam, *Public Lives, Private Secrets*.

29. These controls continued in the nineteenth century to be based both on Roman law and Spanish law, which itself was defined by the thirteenth-century Siete Partidas laws and the sixteenth-century Leyes de Toro.

30. If a notary failed to use the proper caution in this respect, he would be liable for the costs of this illegal transaction, as well as for the damages caused. If he could not cover the costs and damages, he could be suspended for up to two years. See *Código Civil del Estado*, cap. 4: "Los notarios que omitan este requisito incurrirán en la pena de pagar los daños y perjuicios que causaran, y en caso de insolvencia en la suspensión del oficio por dos años."

31. "De las escrituras de contrato; Capitulo I; Art. 7: sobre los contratos de las mujeres casadas: El interés de la sociedad conyugal y la deferencia que la mujer debe a su marido la obligan a no hacer jamás cosa importante sin su licencia ni autorización. No puede por lo tanto la mujer sin licencia del marido hacer contrato, ni separarse del que tuviese hecho, ni estar en juicio demandado ni defendiendo por si o por procurador, ni repudiar herencia por testamento o abintestato, ni aceptarla, sino sólo a beneficio de inventario. Esta licencia se la puede conceder el marido para todos los referidos actos, o sólo especialmente para alguno

de ellos y asimismo puede ratificar lo que hubiere la mujer ejecutado sin su permiso. Si el marido injusta y arbitrariamente se negase a conceder esta licencia a su mujer, puede el juez con conocimiento de causa legítima o necesaria, compelerle que se la otorgue, y si no se la diere, el juez se la puede conceder, pudiéndose ejecutar lo mismo en la propia forma, cuando el marido se halla ausente y no se espera su próxima venida o corre peligro en la tardanza"; see *Novísimo escribano instruido*, sec. 2a, titulo I.

32. Articles similar to article 1779 exist in the 1889 Spanish Civil Code (albeit without the retroactive provision included in the Mexican Civil Code); see articles 62 and 65 of the 1889 Spanish Civil Code.

33. Divorce in this context referred only to a legal separation of residence. Divorced women and men were not free to remarry, and divorce cases were extremely rare before the twentieth century. For more on divorce in Yucatán, see Smith, *Mexican Revolution*.

34. Wives also countersigned loans using joint property as collateral, as the excerpt at the beginning of this chapter illustrates.

35. The civil code presumed the *licencia* (agreement) of the husband when the contract happened in a professional context. The *1866 Código Civil del Imperio Mexicano* states in article 135 of book 1: "La licencia para contratar puede ser general, o especial. Se presume concedida cuando la mujer tiene un establecimiento público o propio, profesional o mercantil, y en ese caso quedan obligados por los contratos relativos al establecimiento, celebrados por la mujer, los bienes del establecimiento mismo; si no bastan, los gananciales del matrimonio y en defecto, los propios de la mujer."

36. Published in 1895, the local census of professional occupations in the city of Mérida suggests that women were largely employed in labores domésticas and 16,854 out of the 27,844 women surveyed were identified as such. The second highest occupation for Mérida women was clothes washers (1,379), none of which appeared identified as such in the mortgage contracts. See *Boletín estadístico*.

37. The sample of sales contracts between 1850 and 1899 amounts to approximately five thousand land sales and deeds.

38. According to the 1895 occupations survey of Mérida, there were twelve sorbet makers in the city. If the business survived for at least five years, Blas Díaz was among them in 1895. See *Boletín estadístico*.

Chapter 6

The epigraph to this chapter is drawn from *Ley del Notariado*, December 29, 1915, cited in *Diccionario histórico*. It reads, "se aumentaron los requisitos para la fe pública, pero se fomentó el monopolio en dicha actividad."

1. Mario Cerutti and Carlos Marichal's edited volume on the development of regional banking in Mexico, *La banca regional*, presents international comparisons and regional microanalyses to make the case that local private credit networks were necessary precursors to the establishment of banks in Mexico.

2. Before the enactment of the notarial code in 1865, notarial students studied civil law and were trained by other notaries in writing and maintaining public documents.

3. This description of educational prerequisites is taken from Bernardo Pérez Fernández del Castillo's *Historia de la escribanía*.

4. The law stipulated a limit on the number of notaries, which could not exceed the number of municipalities in the city, a category that varied during the period from eleven to thirteen municipalities. In 1850 twelve notaries recorded mortgage contracts in Mérida in 1850; for the rest of the period, this number ranged from seven to twelve, accounting for

vacant posts and inactive notaries. Although the *Registro de notarios* registered all notaries when they began their careers, these records have not survived.

5. Cerutti and Marichal, *La banca regional.*

6. The 1896 city directory lists the names and addresses of some one thousand of Mérida's male citizens, including its notaries. It is not clear whether the directory lists the residential or business addresses.

7. See the parish records of APAY and CAIHY.

8. Patrón Zavalegui's death appears in the list of events that marked the year 1907 in Menéndez's historical almanac of Yucatán: "*10 de Julio 1907: Fallece el decano de los notarios de Mérida, don José Anacleto Patrón Zavalegui, que fue muy estimado por su honorabilidad y por su carácter jovial*" (July 10, 1907: Death of José Anacleto Patrón Zavalegui, doyen of the notaries of Mérida. He was much esteemed for his honesty and his jovial character); Menéndez, *90 años de historia,* 220.

9. In the first year a client appeared, he or she was tagged as a new client in the data set. When that same client reappeared in another year, he or she was tagged as an old client. The old and new clients were identified as lenders or borrowers and then divided by the total number of clients in that year. The measure is a conservative one because it does not account for earlier contacts between notary and client for other types of contracts and for years that were not tracked.

10. Mex$214,765 was roughly equivalent to US$170,000 at the time; this is the largest single credit transaction in the sample; see Wells, "All in the Family."

11. Ibid.

12. Francisco Cantón served as Yucatán's governor between 1898 and 1902. As an aside, Cantón had been a supporter of Maximilian in the early 1860s. He later became a strong supporter and ally of Porfirio Díaz, which guaranteed him his post as governor for four years. But he lost Diaz's favor and lost the 1902 elections to Olegario Molina, who was by then the most important henequen trader in Yucatán.

13. Wells, "All in the Family."

14. José Anacleto Patrón Zavalegui, July 30, 1885, libro 393, Fondo Notarios, ANEY.

15. I considered only the clients who interacted with either notary two times or more between 1870 and 1895; a client who made two loans in one year and never again cannot be counted using this method, but this client would also not be able to show a pattern of migration from one notary to the other, which is what I am tracing by using multiple interactions over multiple years.

16. Even the most successful Parisian notary had but a small percentage of the market in Paris; see Hoffman, Postel-Vinay, and Rosenthal, *Priceless Markets.*

Chapter 7

1. Even in the most developed parts of the world, banks do not always operate as they should. The recent banking crisis that started in 2007 and continues into the second decade of the twenty-first century testifies to this.

2. See Cotler, *Entidades microfinancieras*; Esquivel Martínez, "Microfinanzas"; Barrón Pérez, "Microfinanciamiento"; and Terberger, "Microfinance Institutions." For more on problems occurring outside of Latin America, see Yunus, *Banker to the Poor.*

3. The rise of English deposit banks is a clear example of the importance of trust in credit. English deposit banks, like early U.S. investment groups, relied on internal networks between family, coparishioners, and political allies. Personal connections were a sign of personal trust. For the United States, see Lamoreaux, *Insider Lending*; and for England see

Davies, "Country Gentry"; Horsefield, "Stop of the Exchequer"; Joslin, "London Private Bankers"; Laurence, "Emergence"; Melton, *Sir Robert Clayton*; and Temin and Voth, "South Sea Bubble."

4. *Diccionario histórico.*

5. In the first part of *Revolution from Without*, Gilbert Joseph outlines the collusion agreements and tactics between American and Yucatecan henequen traders in the late nineteenth and early twentieth century; see 13–92.

6. Carstensen and Roazen-Parrillo, "Foreign Markets."

Appendix

1. Gómez-Galvarriato and Musacchio, "Nuevo índice."

Bibliography

Archives

Archivo General del Estado de Yucatán (AGEY), Mérida
Archivo Notarial del Estado de Yucatán (ANEY), Mérida
Archivo Parroquial de la Arquidiócesis de Yucatán (APAY), Mérida
Biblioteca Carlos R. Menéndez, Mérida
Biblioteca de la Escuela de Notarios, Mexico City
Biblioteca de la Facultad de Derecho, Universidad Autónoma de Yucatán, Mérida
Centro de Apoyo a la Investigación Histórica de Yucatán (CAIHY), Mérida

Primary Sources

"Balance promedio de bancos." *Boletín estadístico de Mérida: Ocupaciones*. Mérida: CAIHY, 1895.

Castro, D. Juan Miguel. *Informe presentado a la Junta de hacendados y comerciantes, Mérida de Yucatán, 9 de mayo de 1878*. Mérida: Imprenta del comercio a cargo de Ignacio L. Mena.

Código de la Reforma: Nacionalización de bienes eclesiásticos. Vol. 2. Formada y anotada por Licenciado Blas José Gutiérrez Flores Alatorre. Mexico City: Imprenta Constitucional, 1870.

Código Civil del Estado de Yucatán, 1870: Con todas las adiciones y reformas. 3a edición. Mérida, 1885.

Código Civil del Imperio Mexicano. Mexico City: Imprenta de Andrade y Escalante, 1866.

Código Civil Español de 1889. Departamento de Justicia, Generalitat de Catalunya. Accessed July 7, 2011. http://civil.udg.es/normacivil/estatal/cc/indexcc.htm.

Diccionario histórico y bibliográfico de la Revolución Mexicana. Vol. 7. Mexico City: Instituto Nacional de Estudios Históricos sobre la Revoluciones Mexicana, 1992.

Echánove Trujillo, Carlos A., ed. *Enciclopedia yucatánense*. 2nd ed. Mérida: Gobierno del Estado de Yucatán, 1977.

Estadísticas económicas del Porfiriato: Comercio exterior de México, 1877–1911. Mexico City: Colegio de México, 1960.

Ley del Notariado del Estado de Yucatán. *Diario Oficial* (Mexico City), December 12, 1908.

Leyes de la Reforma: Nacionalización de bienes eclesiásticos. Formada y anotada por Licenciado Blas José Gutiérrez Flores Alatorre. Mexico City: Imprenta Constitucional, 1860.

Mason, Gregory. "The Green Gold of Yucatán." *Outlook* 116 (September–December 1916): 822.

Memorias del III Congreso de historia del derecho mexicano. Mexico City: Universidad Nacional Autónoma de México, 1984.

Menéndez, Carlos R. *90 años de historia de Yucatán, 1821–1910*. Mérida: Compañia Tipografica Yucateca, 1937.

El novísimo escribano instruido. 2nd ed. Mexico City, 1892. First printed in 1859. Citations refer to the 1892 edition.

"Principales productos del comercio exterior Mexicano en el siglo XIX." Cuaderno de Trabajo 47. Mexico City: Instituto Nacional de Antropología e Historia, 1985.

Secondary Sources

Abreu-Gómez, Ermilo. *La conjura de Xincum: La Guerra de Castas en Yucatán.* Mérida: Maldonado Editores, 1983.

Alston, Lee, Shannan Mattiace, and Thomas Nonnenmacher. "Coercion, Culture, and Contracts: Labor and Debt on Henequen Haciendas in Yucatán, Mexico, 1870–1915." *Journal of Economic History* 69 (2009): 104–37.

Ariely, Dan. *Predictably Irrational: The Hidden Forces That Shape Our Decisions.* New York: Harper Collins, 2008.

Arrom, Silvia Marina. "Changes in Mexican Family Law in the Nineteenth Century." In *Confronting Change, Challenging Tradition: Women in Latin American History,* edited by Gertrude M. Yeager, 87–102. Wilmington, Del.: Scholarly Resources, 1994.

———. *The Women of Mexico City, 1790–1857.* Palo Alto: Stanford University Press, 1985.

Baqueiro, Serapio. *Ensayo histórico de las revoluciones de Yucatán desde al año de 1840 hasta 1864.* Mérida: Imprenta de Heredia Argüelles, 1878. First published 1873 by Imprenta Literaría dirigida por Canto. Microfilm available at Miami University Libraries. Accessed July 11, 2011. http://www.lib.muohio.edu/multifacet/record/mu3ugb1157659.

———. "Reseña geográfica, histórica, y estadística del Estado de Yucatán desde los primitivos tiempos de la península, México, 1881." In *Geografía política de Yucatán 1821–1900,* edited by Salvador Rodríguez Losa. Mérida: Universidad Autónoma de Yucatán, 1989.

Barickman, Bert Jude. *A Bahian Counterpoint: Sugar, Tobacco, Cassava, and Slavery in the Reconcavo, 1780–1860.* Palo Alto: Stanford University Press, 1998.

Barrón Pérez, María Antonieta. "Microfinanciamiento y reducción de la pobreza: Fondos Regionales Indígenas." *Problemas del Desarrollo* 34, no. 134 (2003): 126–48.

Beatty, Edward. *Institutions and Investment: The Political Basis of Industrialization in Mexico Before 1911.* Palo Alto: Stanford University Press, 2001.

Bell, Clive, T. N. Srinivasan, and Christopher Udry. "Rationing, Spillover, and Interlinking Credit Markets: The Case of Rural Punjab." *Oxford Economic Papers* 49, no. 4 (1997): 557–85.

Besley, Timothy, and Alec Levenson. "The Role of Informal Finance in Household Capital Accumulation: Evidence from Taiwan." *Economic Journal* 106, no. 434 (1996): 39–59.

Bojórquez Urzaiz, Carlos E. *La emigración cubana en Yucatán, 1868–1898.* Mérida: Imagen Contemporánea, 2000.

Borja Martínez, Manuel. "La usura en el Código de 1870." *Jurídica* 3 (July 1971): 218–39.

Botticini, Maristella. "A Tale of 'Benevolent' Governments: Private Credit, Public Finance, and the Role of Jewish Lenders in Medieval and Renaissance Italy." *Journal of Economic History* 60, no. 1 (2000): 164–89.

Bottin, Jacques, Pierre Jeannin, and Marie-Louise Pelus. *Marchands d'Europe: Pratiques et savoirs à l'époque moderne.* Paris: Editions Rue d'Ulm, 2002.

Boyer, Richard E. *Lives of the Bigamists: Marriage, Family, and Community in Colonial Mexico.* Albuquerque: University of New Mexico Press, 1995.

Brading, David A. *Miners and Merchants in Bourbon Mexico, 1873–1810.* Cambridge: Cambridge University Press, 1971.

Brannon, Jeffery. *Agrarian Reform and Public Enterprise in Mexico: The Political Economy of Yucatán's Henequen Industry*. Tuscaloosa: University of Alabama Press, 1987.

Burns, Kathryn. *Colonial Habits: Convents and the Spiritual Economy of Cuzco, Peru*. Durham: Duke University Press, 1999.

Caplan, Karen. *Indigenous Citizens: Local Liberalism in Early National Oaxaca and Yucatan*. Palo Alto: Stanford University Press, 2010.

Cardenas, Enrique. "A Macroeconomic Interpretation of Nineteenth-Century Mexico." In *How Latin American Fell Behind: Essays on the Economic Histories of Brazil and Mexico, 1800–1914*, edited by Steve Haber, 65–92. Palo Alto: Stanford University Press, 1997.

Carrillo, Luis. *Secretos de familia: Libaneses y élites empresariales en Yucatán*. Mexico City: Conaculta, 1994.

Carstensen, Fred, and Diane Roazen-Parrillo. "Foreign Markets, Domestic Initiative, and the Emergence of a Monocrop Economy: The Yucatecan Experience." *Hispanic American Historical Review* 72, no. 4 (1992): 555–92.

Cerutti, Mario, and Carlos Marichal, eds. *La banca regional en México, 1870–1930*. Mexico City: Fondo de Cultura Económica, 2003.

Chamoux, Marie-Noëlle, Daniele Dehouve, Cecile Gouy-Gilbert, and Marielle Pepin Lehalleur, eds. *Prêter et emprunter: Pratiques de credit au Mexique*. Paris: Editions de la Maison de Sciences de L'homme, 1993.

Chowning, Margaret. "The consolidación de vales reales in the bishopric of Michoacán." *Hispanic American Historical Review* 69, no. 3 (1989): 451–78.

———. *Wealth and Power in Provincial Mexico: Michoacán from the Late Colony to the Revolution*. Stanford: Stanford University Press, 1999.

Coatsworth, John H. *Growth Against Development: The Economic Impact of Railroads in Porfirian Mexico*. De Kalb: Northern Illinois University Press, 1981.

———. "Obstacles to Economic Growth in Nineteenth-Century Mexico." *American Historical Review* 83 (1978): 80–100.

Cotler, Pablo. *Las entidades microfinancieras del México urbano*. Mexico City: Universidad Iberoamericana, 2003.

Cunningham, Michelle. *Mexico and the Foreign Policies of Napoleon III*. New York: Palgrave, 2001.

Dabbs, Jack Autrey. *The French Army in Mexico, 1861–1897*. The Hague: Mouton, 1963.

Davies, Margaret Gay. "Country Gentry and Payments to London, 1650–1714." *Economic History Review* 24 (1971): 15–36.

Deere, Carmen Diana, and Magdalena León. *Empowering Women: Land and Property Rights in Latin America*. Pittsburgh: Pittsburgh University Press, 2001.

———. "Liberalism and Married Women's Property Rights in Nineteenth-Century Latin America." *Hispanic American Historical Review* 85, no. 4 (2005): 627–78.

Del Ángel-Mobarak, Gustavo. "Paradoxes of Financial Development: The Construction of the Mexican Banking System, 1941–1982." PhD diss., Stanford University, 2002.

De Soto, Hernando. *The Other Path*. New York: Basic Books, 1989.

Dumond, Don E. *The Machete and the Cross: Campesino Rebellion in Yucatán*. Lincoln: University of Nebraska Press, 1997.

Dumond, Don E., and Carol Streichen Dumond, eds. "Demography and Parish Affairs in the Yucatán, 1767–1897." Working paper, University of Oregon, 1982.

Dye, Alan. *Cuban Sugar in the Age of Mass Production: Technology and the Economy of the Sugar Central, 1899–1929*. Palo Alto: Stanford University Press, 1998.

Engermann, Stanley, and Kenneth Sokoloff. "History Lessons: Institutions, Factor Endowments, and Paths of Development in the New World." *Journal of Economic Perspectives* 14, no. 3 (2000): 217–32.

Ensminger, Jean. *Making a Market: The Institutionalization of an African Society.* Cambridge: Cambridge University Press, 1996.

Esquivel Martínez, Horacio. "Las microfinanzas como respuesta a la información asimétrica: El caso de la ciudad de México." *Comercio Exterior* 56, no. 8 (2006): 658–72.

Evans, Sterling. *Bound in Twine: The History and Ecology of the Henequen-Wheat Complex for Mexico and the American and Canadian Plains, 1880–1950.* College Station: Texas A&M, 2007.

Farriss, Nancy. *Maya Society Under Colonial Rule: The Collective Enterprise of Survival.* Princeton: Princeton University Press, 1984.

Finn, Margot C. *The Character of Credit: Personal Debt in English Culture, 1740–1914.* Cambridge: Cambridge University Press, 2003.

Florescano, Enrique, and Isabel Gil Sánchez. *La época del las reformas borbónicas y del crecimiento económico, 1750–1808.* Mexico City: Instituto Nacional de Antropología e Historia, 1974.

Fohlin, Caroline. "Universal Banking in Pre–World War I Germany: Model or Myth?" *Explorations in Economic History* 36 (1999): 305–43.

Francesca, Ersilia. "Merchants and Money: Formal and Informal Credit Networks as Alternative Basis for Interest in Medieval Islam." Paper presented at the World Economic History Conference, Utrecht, August 2009.

François, Marie Eileen. *A Culture of Everyday Credit: Housekeeping, Pawnbroking, and Governance in Mexico City, 1750–1920.* Lincoln: University of Nebraska Press, 2006.

Frank, Zephyr. *Dutra's World: Wealth and Family in Nineteenth-Century Rio de Janeiro.* Albuquerque: University of New Mexico Press, 2004.

Franklin, Sarah, and Susan McKinnon, eds. *Relative Values: Reconfiguring Kinship Studies.* Durham: Duke University Press, 2001.

Gauderman, Kimberly. *Women's Lives in Colonial Quito: Gender, Law, and Economy in Spanish America.* Austin: University of Texas Press, 2003.

Gay, Suzanne. *The Moneylenders of Late Medieval Kyoto.* Honolulu: University of Hawai'i Press, 2001.

Geertz, Clifford. *Peddlers and Princes: Social Development and Economic Change in Two Indonesian Towns.* Chicago: University of Chicago Press, 1963.

Gómez-Galvarriato, Aurora, and Aldo Musacchio. "Un nuevo índice de precios para México, 1886–1929." *Trimestre Económico* 67 (January–March 2000): 47–91.

González Navarro, Moisés. *Raza y tierra: La Guerra de Castas y el henequén.* Mexico City: Colegio de México, 1970.

Granovetter, Mark. "The Strength of Weak Ties." *American Journal of Sociology* 78, no. 6 (1973): 1360–80.

Greenow, Linda. *Credit and Socioeconomic Change in Colonial Mexico: Loans and Mortgages in Guadalajara, 1720–1820.* Boulder: Westview Press, 1982.

Greif, Avner. "Contract Enforceability and Economic Institutions in Early Trade: The Maghribi Traders' Coalition." *American Economic Review* 83, no. 3 (1993): 525–48.

Guinnane, Timothy W. "Cooperatives as Information Machines: German Rural Credit Cooperatives, 1883–1914." *Journal of Economic History* 61, no. 2 (2001): 366–92.

Haber, Stephen, ed. *Crony Capitalism and Economic Growth in Latin America: Theory and Evidence.* Chicago: Hoover Press, 2002.

———. "Financial Markets and Industrial Development: A Comparative Study of Governmental Regulation, Financial Innovation, and Industrial Structure in Brazil and Mexico, 1840–1930" In *How Latin America Fell Behind: Essays on the Economic Histo-*

ries of Brazil and Mexico, 1800–1914, edited by Stephen Haber, 146–78. Palo Alto: Stanford University Press, 1997.

———. "Industrial Concentration and the Capital Markets: A Comparative Study of Brazil, Mexico, and the United States, 1830–1930." *Journal of Economic History* 51, no. 3 (1991) 559–80.

———. *Industry and Underdevelopment: The Industrialization of Mexico, 1890–1949*. Stanford: Stanford University Press, 1989.

———. "The Political Economy of Latin American Industrialization." In *The Long Twentieth Century*. Vol. 2 of *The Cambridge Economic History of Latin America*, edited by Victor Bulmer-Thomas, John Coatsworth, and Roberto Cortes Conde, 537–84. Cambridge: Cambridge University Press, 2006.

Haber, Stephen, Armando Razo, and Noel Maurer. *The Politics of Property Rights: Political Instability, Credible Commitments, and Economic Growth in Mexico, 1876–1929*. Cambridge: Cambridge University Press, 2003.

Hamilton, Sarah. "Neoliberalism, Gender, and Property Rights in Rural Mexico." *Latin American Research Review* 37, no. 1 (2002): 119–43.

Hamnett, Brian R. "The Appropriation of Mexican Church Wealth by the Spanish Bourbon Government: The 'Consolidación de Vales Reales,' 1805–1809," *Journal of Latin American Studies* 1 (1969): 85–113.

———. *Politics and Trade in Southern México, 1750–1821*. Cambridge: Cambridge University Press, 1971.

Hanley, Anne. *Native Capital: Financial Institutions and Economic Development in São Paulo, Brazil 1850–1920*. Stanford: Stanford University Press, 2005.

Hanson-Jones, Alice. *Wealth of a Nation to Be: The American Colonies on the Eve of the Revolution*. New York: Columbia University Press, 1980.

Hardwick, Julie. *The Practice of Patriarchy: Gender and the Politics of Household Authority in Early Modern France*. University Park: Pennsylvania State University Press, 1998.

Hoffman, Philip T., Gilles Postel-Vinay, and Jean-Laurent Rosenthal. *Priceless Markets: The Political Economy of Credit in Paris, 1660–1870*. Chicago: University of Chicago Press, 2000.

Horsefield, J. Keith. "The 'Stop of the Exchequer' Revisited." *Economic History Review* 35 (1982): 511–28.

Hu-De Hart, Evelyn. *Yaqui Resistance and Survival: Struggle for Land and Autonomy, 1821–1910*. Madison: University of Wisconsin Press, 1984.

Joseph, Gilbert M. *Rediscovering the Past at Mexico's Periphery: Essays on the History of Modern Yucatán*. Tuscaloosa: University of Alabama Press, 1986.

———. *Revolution from Without: Yucatán, Mexico, and the United States, 1880–1924*. Durham: Duke University Press, 1988.

Joseph, Gilbert, and Allen Wells. *Summer of Discontent, Seasons of Upheaval: Elite Politics and Rural Insurgency in Yucatán, 1876–1915*. Palo Alto: Stanford University Press, 1996.

Joslin, D. M. "London Private Bankers, 1720–1785." *Economic History Review* 7 (1954): 167–86.

Katz, Friedrich. *Pancho Villa: His Life and Times*. Palo Alto: Stanford University Press, 1998.

Kinsbrunner, Jay. *Independence in Spanish America: Civil Wars, Revolutions, and Underdevelopment*. Albuquerque: University of New Mexico Press, 2000.

Knight, Alan. *The Mexican Revolution*. 2 vols. Cambridge: Cambridge University Press, 1986.

Korth, Eugene H., and Della M. Flusche. "Dowry and Inheritance in Colonial Spanish America: Peninsular Law and Chilean Practice." *Americas* 43, no. 4 (1987): 395–410.

Lamoreaux, Noami. *Insider Lending: Banks, Personal Connections, and Economic Development in Industrial New England.* Cambridge: Cambridge University Press, 1996.

Lapointe, Marie. *Los Mayas rebeldes de Yucatán.* Zamora, Michoacán: Colegio de Michoacán, 1983.

Laurence, Anne. "The Emergence of a Private Clientele for Banks in the Early Eighteenth Century: Hoare's Bank and Some Women Customers." *Economic History Review* 61 (2008): 565–86.

Lavrin, Asunción. "The Execution of the Law of Consolidation in New Spain: Economic Aims and Results." *Hispanic American Historical Review* 53, no. 1 (1973): 27–49.

Le Goff, Jacques. *Your Money or Your Life: Economy and Religion in the Middle Ages.* New York: Zone Books, 1988.

LeGrand, Catherine, and Adriana Mercedes Corso. "Los archivos notariales como fuente histórica: Una perspectiva desde la zona bananera del Magdalena (Colombia)." *Anuario Colombiano de Historia Social y de la Cultura* 31 (2004): 159–208.

Lemercier, Claire. "L'institution et le groupe: Logiques, strategies, territoires—Devenir une institution locale: La Chambre de commerce de Paris au XIXe siecle." *Revue d'histoire moderne et contemporaine* 54, no. 3 (2007): 40.

———. *Un si discret pouvoir: Aux origines de la Chambre de Commerce de Paris, 1803–1853.* Paris: Découverte, 2003.

Levenson, Alec, and William Maloney. "The Informal Sector, Firm Dynamics, and Institutional Participation." World Bank Policy Research Working Paper, Washington, DC, 1998.

Levine, Ross. "Financial Development and Economic Growth: Views and Agenda." *Journal of Economic Literature* 35 (1997): 688–726.

Lockhart, James. *The First Men of Cajamarca: A Social and Biographical Study of the First Conquerors of Peru.* Austin: University of Texas Press, 1972.

Luckett, Thomas. "Credit and Commercial Society in France, 1740–1789." PhD diss., Princeton University, 1992.

Ludlow, Leonor, and Carlos Marichal, eds. *Banca y poder en México, 1800–1925.* Mexico City: Editorial Grijalbo, 1985.

Lutz, Wolfgang, Leonel Prieto, and Warren Sanderson, eds. *Population, Development, and Environment on the Yucatan Peninsula, from Ancient Maya to 2030.* Laxenburg, Austria: International Institute for Applied Systems Analysis, 2000.

Lynch, John. *Bourbon Spain, 1700–1808.* New York: Wiley and Sons, 1994.

MacMillan, John, and Chris Woodruff. "Interfirm Relationships and Informal Credit in Vietnam." *Quarterly Journal of Economics* 114 (November 2000): 1285–320.

Marichal, Carlos, coord. *Las inversiones extranjeras en América Latina, 1850–1930.* Mexico City: Fondo de Cultural Económica, 1995.

———. "Obstacles to the Development of Capital Markets in Nineteenth-Century Mexico." In *How Latin America Fell Behind*, edited by Stephen Haber, 118–45. Palo Alto: Stanford University Press, 1997.

Marquez, Graciela. "Tariff Protection in Mexico, 1892–1910: Ad Valorem Tariff Rates and Sources of Variation." In *Latin America and the World Economy Since 1800*, edited by John H. Coatsworth and Alan M. Taylor, 407–42. Cambridge: Harvard University Press, 1998.

Maurer, Noel. *The Power and the Money: The Mexican Financial System, 1876–1932.* Palo Alto: Stanford University Press, 2002.

Melton, Frank T. *Sir Robert Clayton and the Origins of English Deposit Banking, 1658–1685.* Cambridge: Cambridge University Press, 1986.

Merwick, Donna. *Death of a Notary: Conquest and Change in Colonial New York*. Ithaca: Cornell University Press, 1999.

Mirow, Matthew C. *Latin American Law: A History of Private Law and Institutions in Spanish America*. Austin: University of Texas Press, 2004.

Moreno Fraginals, Manuel. *El ingenio: Complejo económico social cubano del azúcar*. Havana: Ciencias Sociales, 1978.

Musacchio, Aldo. *Experiments in Financial Democracy: Corporate Governance and Financial Development in Brazil, 1882–1950*. Cambridge: Cambridge University Press, 2010.

Nazzari, Muriel. *Disappearance of the Dowry: Women, Families, and Social Change in São Paulo, Brazil, 1600–1900*. Palo Alto: Stanford University Press, 1991.

Nelson, Benjamin. *The Idea of Usury, from Tribal Brotherhood to Universal Otherhood*. Chicago: University of Chicago Press, 1969.

Noonan, John T., Jr. *The Scholastic Analysis of Usury*. Cambridge: Harvard University Press, 1957.

North, Douglass. *Institutions, Institutional Change, and Economic Performance*. Cambridge: Cambridge University Press, 1990.

North, Douglass, and Robert Paul Thomas. *The Rise of the Western World: A New Economic History*. Cambridge: Cambridge University Press, 1976.

Olegario, Rowena. *A Culture of Credit: Embedding Trust and Transparency in American Business*. Cambridge: Harvard University Press, 2006.

Ota Mishima, María Elena. *Destino México: Un estudio de las migraciones asiáticas a México, siglos XIX y XX*. Mexico City: Colegio de México, 1997.

Patch, Robert. *Maya and Spaniard in Yucatán, 1648–1812*. Stanford: Stanford University Press, 1994.

Peniche Rivero, Piedad. "La comunidad doméstica en la hacienda henequenera de Yucatán, 1870–1915." *Mexican Studies/Estudios Mexicanos* 15, no. 1 (1999): 1–33.

Pérez Fernández del Castillo, Bernardo. *Apuntes para la historia del notariado en México*. Mexico City: Fundación Nacional del Notariado Mexicano, 1979.

———. *Historia de la escribanía en la Nueva España y del notariado en México*. Ed. Porrúa. Mexico City: Colegio de Notarios del Distrito Federal, 1988.

Pérez Sarmiento, Marisa, coord. *El cultivo de las élites: Grupos económicos y políticos en Yucatán en los siglos XIX y XX*. Mexico City: Conaculta, 2001.

Quezada, Sergio. *Pueblos y caciques yucatecos, 1550–1580*. Mexico City: Colegio de México, 1993.

Recio, Gabriela. "El abogado y la empresa: Una mirada a los negocios posrevolucionarios, 1925–1945." PhD diss., Colegio de México, 2008.

Reed, Nelson. *The Caste War of Yucatán*. Palo Alto: Stanford University Press, 1964.

Remmers, Lawrence. "Henequen: The Caste War and the Economy of Yucatán, 1846–1883; The Roots of Dependence in a Mexican Region." PhD diss., University of California, Los Angeles, 1981.

Restall, Matthew. *Maya World: Yucatec Culture and Society, 1550–1850*. Palo Alto: Stanford University Press, 1999.

Ridings, Eugene. *Business Interest Groups in Nineteenth-Century Brazil*. Cambridge: Cambridge University Press, 2004.

Roberts, Bryan. *Economic Origins of Dictatorship and Democracy*. Cambridge: Cambridge University Press, 2005.

———. "Informal Economy and Family Strategies." *International Journal of Urban and Regional Research* 18, no. 1 (1994): 6–23.

Robinson, James A., and Daron Acemoglu. "Economic Backwardness in Political Perspective." *American Political Science Review* 100, no. 1 (2006): 115–31.

Rockoff, Hugh. "Prodigals and Projectors: An Economic History of Usury Laws in the United States from Colonial Times to 1900." In *Human Capital and Institutions: A*

Long-Run View, edited by David Eltis, Frank Lewis, and Kenneth Sokoloff, 284–324. Cambridge: Cambridge University Press, 2009.

Rodríguez Losa, Salvador, ed. *Geografía política de Yucatán, 1821–1900.* Mérida: Universidad Autónoma de Yucatán, 1989.

Rosenthal, Jean-Laurent. "Credit Markets and Economic Change in Southeastern France, 1630–1788." *Explorations in Economic History* 30 (April 1993): 129–57.

Rugeley, Terry, ed. *Maya Wars: Ethnographic Accounts from Nineteenth-Century Yucatán.* Norman: University of Oklahoma Press, 2001.

———. *Of Wonders and Wise Men: Religion and Popular Cultures in Southeast Mexico, 1800–1876.* Austin: University of Texas Press, 2001.

———. *Yucatán's Maya Peasantry and the Origins of the Caste War.* Austin: University of Texas Press, 1996.

Sánchez Novelo, Faulo. *La recreación en Yucatán durante el Segundo Imperio (1864–1867).* Mérida: Maldonado Editores del Mayab, 1999.

Saragoza, Alex. *The Monterrey Elite and the Mexican State, 1880–1940.* Austin: University of Texas Press, 1998.

Seed, Patricia. *To Love, Honor, and Obey in Colonial Mexico: Conflicts over Marriage Choice, 1574–1821.* Palo Alto: Stanford University Press, 1988.

Smith, Stephanie. *Gender and the Mexican Revolution: Yucatán Women and the Realities of Patriarchy.* Chapel Hill: University of North Carolina Press, 2009.

Socolow, Susan Midgen. *The Women of Colonial Latin America.* Cambridge: Cambridge University Press, 2000.

Stephen, Quinn. "Goldsmith-Banking: Mutual Acceptance and Interbanker Clearing in Restoration London." *Explorations in Economic History* 34 (1997): 411–32.

Suárez Molina, Víctor. *La evolución económica de Yucatán a través del siglo XIX.* Mérida: Universidad Autónoma de Yucatán, 1977.

Sudhanshu, Handa, and Kirton Claremont. "The Economics of Rotating Savings and Credit Associations: Evidence from the Jamaican Partner." *Journal of Development Economics* 60, no. 1 (1999): 173–94.

Sweigart, Joseph. "Financing and Marketing Brazilian Export Agriculture: The Coffee Factors of Rio de Janeiro, 1850–1888." PhD diss., University of Texas, Austin, 1980.

Tan, Elaine. "An Empty Shell? Rethinking the Usury Laws in Medieval Europe." *Journal of Legal History* 23, no. 3 (2001): 177–96.

———. "The Usury Prohibition, 1100–1400: A Study in the New Institutional Economic History." PhD diss., Cambridge University, 2001.

Taylor, John Metcalf. *Maximilian and Carlotta: A Story of Imperialism.* New York: Putnam and Sons, 1894.

Taylor, William B. *Magistrates of the Sacred: Priests and Parishioners in Eighteenth-Century Mexico.* Stanford: Stanford University Press, 1999.

Temin, Peter, and Hans Joachim Voth. "Financial Repression in a Natural Experiment: Loan Allocation and the Change in the Usury Laws in 1714." Discussion Paper No. 4452, Center for Economic and Policy Research, Washington, DC, 2004.

———. "Riding the South Sea Bubble." *American Economic Review* 94, no. 5 (2004): 1654–68.

Tenenbaum, Barbara. *The Politics of Penury: Debt and Taxes in Mexico, 1821–1856.* Albuquerque: University of New Mexico Press, 1986.

Terberger, Eva. "Microfinance Institutions in the Development of Financial Markets." *CEPAL Review* 81 (December 2003): 187–202.

Triner, Gail. *Banking and Economic Development: Brazil, 1889–1930.* New York: Palgrave Press, 2000.

Turner, John Kenneth. *Barbarous Mexico.* Chicago: Kerr, 1911.

Twinam, Ann. *Public Lives, Private Secrets: Gender, Honor, Sexuality, and Illegitimacy in Colonial Spanish America*. Palo Alto: Stanford University Press, 1999.

Van Bochove, Christiaan. "Intermediaries and the Secondary Market for Government Bonds in the Dutch Republic." Paper presented at the workshop on Intermediaries and Intermediation in Capital Markets: A Global Historical Approach, Utrecht University, June 2010.

Van Hoy, Teresa. *A Social History of Mexico's Railroads: Peons, Prisoners, and Priests*. Rowman and Littlefield, 2008.

Van Young, Eric. *Hacienda and Market in Eighteenth-Century Mexico: The Rural Economy of the Guadalajara Region, 1675–1820*. Berkeley: University of California Press, 1981.

———, ed. *Mexican Regions: Comparative History and Development*. La Jolla: Center for U.S.-Mexican Studies, University of California, San Diego, 1992.

———. *The Other Rebellion: Popular Violence, Ideology, and the Mexican Struggle for Independence, 1810–1821*. Palo Alto: Stanford University Press, 2001.

Veblen, Thorstein. *The Theory of the Leisure Class*. 1899. Reprint, Oxford: Oxford University Press, 2008.

Von Wobeser, Gisela. *El crédito eclesiástico en la Nueva España, siglo XVIII*. Mexico City: Instituto de Investigaciones Históricas, Universidad Nacional Autónoma de México, 1994.

Walker, David. *Kinship, Business, and Politics: The Martinez del Rio Family in Mexico, 1824–1867*. Latin American Monographs 70. Austin: University of Texas, 1986.

Walton, Clifford Stevens. *The Civil Law in Spain and Spanish-America*. Washington, DC: Lowdermilk, 1900.

Wasserman, Mark. *Capitalists, Caciques, and Revolution: The Native Elite and Foreign Enterprise in Chihuahua, Mexico, 1854–1911*. Chapel Hill: North Carolina University Press, 1984.

Wells, Allen. "All in the Family: Railroads and Henequen Monoculture in Porfirian Yucatan." *Hispanic American Historical Review* 65, no. 3 (1992): 159–209.

———. *Yucatán's Gilded Age: Haciendas, Henequen, and International Harvester, 1860–1915*. Albuquerque: University of New Mexico Press, 1985.

Wiemers, Eugene. "Agriculture and Credit in Nineteenth-Century Mexico: Orizaba and Cordoba, 1822–71." *Hispanic American Historical Review* 65, no. 3 (1985): 519–46.

Womack, John. *Zapata and the Mexican Revolution*. New York: Vintage, 1970.

Yunus, Muhammad. *Banker to the Poor: Micro-lending and the Battle Against World Poverty*. New York: Public Affairs, 1999.

Zucker, Lynne. "Production of Trust: Institutional Sources of Economic Structure, 1840–1920." *Research in Organizational Behavior* 8 (1986): 53–111.

Index

Greif, Avner, 135 nn. 2, 6
Guzman de Quijano, María Encarnación, 91
Guzman, Eligio, 81, 113

haciendas
    accounts and, 46, 49–52
    employee debts on, 46, 49
    private debts on, 46
    probates and, 46, 49–53
henequen
    as binding twine, 1, 26, 28
    credit and, 17, 26, 59 (see also credit)
    and credit markets, 17, 18, 28, 30
    and debt peonage, 48, 49–51
    demise of, 128
    drying of, 25, 26
    export of, 16, 23, 24–25
    financing, 25, 48
    harvesting, 25, 46
    labor force and, 30, 48, 71, 125
    land values and, 59
    Maya labor and, 27, 31, 49, 51, 53
    mortgages and, 84, 85
    as naval cordage, 1, 23
    plantations, 4, 25–26, 28, 128
    planting, 4, 5
    prices, 128
    production of, 24–26
    technology and, 20, 25 (see also innovation,
        in technology; railroads)
Hoffman, Philip, 11,135, 137, 142, 147

inequality
    and credit market effect, 31–33
    and Mayas 31–33 (see also Mayas)
informal credit markets. See credit, informal
information
    asymmetric, 70
    flows, 65–66, 109, 126
    and intermediation, 71–74, 111, 115, 125–27
    lender's need for, 70, 126
    notaries' access to, 78, 83–84, 125–26
    and risk assessment, 97
inheritance, 87, 98
    and equal partible inheritance rules, 99–100
    and laws about, 14, 15, 16, 20, 27, 144 n. 13
    testamentary tradition, 91, 144 n. 14
    and women, 86, 89, 90, 99, 143 nn. 7, 27
innovation
    in credit markets, 3–5, 11, 109
    in technology, 20, 25–26, 27
institutions
    and capital markets, 2, 3

and credit markets, 3, 8, 39
and economic growth, 3, 4, 5, 47, 128
and notaries, 2, 5, 6
types of, 2, 4, 5, 7
interest rates
    banks and, 47
    borrower behavior and, 97
    ecclesiastical/canon law, 35–36, 39, 144 n.
        22
    disparities between men and women in, 95–
        98
    implicit, 45, 46
    kin and, 67
    mortgages and, 41–46
    reforms related to, 39, 40–41, 42
    rise in, 39, 40, 45
    usury and, 39, 42–46
intermediaries, financial, 1
    banks and, 124, 135 n. 1
    information for, 13, 71, 125
    notaries as, 2, 5–6, 7, 13, 45, 66, 108, 125,
        135 n. 1
    types of, 1, 5, 7, 8, 124
International Harvester Company, 26, 128
investments, 3, 4, 27
IOUs (pagarés), 46, 54. See also credit, short-
    term

Juárez, Benito, 22, 34–38, 59

kinship, 9, 10, 82
    and credit, 9, 67–69, 71
    and loan repayments, 68
    See also interest rates

Lamoreaux, Naomi, ix, 141 n. 17, 147 n. 3
lawyers, 11, 56, 66
legal system
    and colonial inheritance, 89, 143 n. 7,
        145 n. 27
    and Siete Partidas, 88, 145 n. 29
    and Roman law, 55, 88
legislation
    credit (see Reform War and Reform Laws)
    credit market and, 13, 39, 41, 42, 43–44,
        58–59
lenders
    behavior of, 70, 72, 73, 76
    characteristics of, 33, 74
    dependence on notaries by, 59, 66
    henequen and, 84
    loyalty to notaries by, 74–81
    motivations of, 70, 84